D0708577

Depression
Your Questions Answered

Dr Melvyn Lurie

LONDON, NEW YORK, MUNICH, MELBOURNE, DELHI

DORLING KINDERSLEY
Editor Tom Broder
Senior Art Editor Nicola Rodway
Executive Managing Editor Adèle Hayward
Managing Art Editor Nick Harris
DTP Designer Traci Salter
Production Controller Clare Mclean
Art Director Peter Luff
Publisher Corinne Roberts

DK INDIA
Senior Editor Dipali Singh
Project Editor Rohan Sinha
Editors Ankush Saikia, Aakriti Singhal
Project Designer Romi Chakraborty
DTP Coordinator Pankaj Sharma
DTP Designer Balwant Singh,
Sunil Sharma
Head of Publishing Aparna Sharma

Edited for Dorling Kindersley by
Kesta Desmond and Philip Morgan

This edition first published in the United Kingdom in 2007 by
Dorling Kindersley Limited, 80 Strand, London WC2R 0RL
A Penguin Company

2 4 6 8 10 9 7 5 3 1

A CIP catalogue record for this book is available from the British Library.

ISBN: 978-1-4053-1757-3

Printed and bound in Singapore by Tien Wah Press

See our complete catalogue at
www.dk.com

Foreword

Depression is a debilitating disease that affects many millions of people worldwide. I have written this book because I have learned from my depressed patients and their families how much better they do when they know exactly what they are dealing with. I feel certain that readers of this book who are suffering from depression and their families will also do better from knowing the answers to the questions addressed in this book.

I have tried to address the most common questions and to make my answers as accessible and comprehensible as possible, while maintaining the accuracy of the information. What I hope readers gain is a general idea of what depression is, and is not, and how it affects people in their everyday lives. I describe the various subtypes, as there are many varieties of depression, and present an overview of the most common treatments, from self-help through to psychological and medical treatments.

Depression drains life of vitality. I hope that the knowledge in this book will help people regain it.

Melvyn Lurie

Dr Melvyn Lurie

Contents

What is depression?

Depression can be a confusing term, as there are several different kinds. The simplest kind is the normal reaction we all have to disappointment; we feel down or blue. However, if the feeling lasts longer than a couple of weeks, is intense, accompanied by certain symptoms, or interferes significantly with our lives, we might have one of the conditions that are known collectively as depression.

Understanding depression

Q How many people have depression?

Very many people – about 5–10 per cent of the population – have a major depression at any given point in time, and it is estimated that 15 per cent of people will develop a major depression some time in their lives.

Q When does feeling blue cross the line into depression?

When you feel so low that you cannot concentrate on anything else, such as work or family obligations, or if you are feeling suicidal, then the line has been crossed. You are also likely to be depressed if low mood lasts for over 2 weeks or if your sleep, appetite, energy, and thoughts are affected for that long, as well as your mood.

Q Is sadness a characteristic of depression?

Sometimes. However, sadness is different from depression. Sadness does not imply feeling disinterested, whereas depression often does. In fact, when someone is sad, he or she is often quite interested in what led to the sadness. The same goes for grief. As painful as it is, grief – as well as its less intense counterpart, bereavement – does not imply depression. Some grieving or bereaved people may develop depression, but this is generally not the case. To understand depression it is just as important to know what it is not, as what it is.

Q What makes one person's depression different from another's?

Depressions differ in terms of their intensity, duration, and the breadth of symptoms involved. There are also different types of depression – some are more biological in origin, while others are more related to stressful life events.

Q **What are the different types of depression?**

You may become depressed in reaction to a stressful event in your life, such as losing your job or a relationship. This type of depression is described as an adjustment disorder with depressed mood (or reactive depression). Its symptoms tend to be comparatively few or mild, but nevertheless, they can sometimes include intensely depressed mood or suicidal behaviour, which means this depression should not be ignored. Another type of depression is major depressive disorder (previously called major affective disorder or unipolar depression), which is more biological in origin. Major depressive disorder is characterized by major depressive episodes. The symptoms of this disorder tend to be greater and more severe than those of adjustment disorder (see below).

Q **Are there any other types?**

There are other types of depressions with major depressive episodes, and these include depression in bipolar disorder (previously called manic-depressive disease) and postnatal depression. Major depressive disorder and other depressions with major depressive episodes are the types of depression that are most responsive to antidepressant medication.

Q **Which kind of depression is the most common?**

Adjustment disorder with depressed mood is the most common type of depression. This condition is triggered by stress, usually due to a sudden event, such as the loss of a job or break-up of a relationship. The death of a loved one can also trigger adjustment disorder with depressed mood. However, this is far from inevitable – many people experience normal states of grief and bereavement without becoming depressed.

Q **What makes depression come and go?**

The cause of a condition is generally something that eliminates it if reversed. The trigger is generally a final event. If you are vulnerable to depression, various factors can trigger it. For example, in postnatal depression (depression following childbirth), the trigger is labour and delivery; in major depressive disorder, the trigger can be social or psychological stress – even quite mild stress – in combination with a person's biology. Depression usually resolves with time, with treatment, or with a lessening of the stress or life event that triggered the depression in the first place. Sometimes, however, depressive episodes don't go away and depression becomes chronic. There might be ways to lessen the pain, there might be good and bad days, but overall, in these cases the bulk of the depressive symptoms remain.

Q **Does stress always trigger depressive episodes?**

Not always. Even a clear, intense source of stress can lead to different reactions in different people and it is hard to predict exactly how an individual will react to stress. Someone with major depressive disorder might react by having a major depressive episode. Someone else might react with an adjustment disorder with depressed mood. Yet another person might react by feeling depressed for a matter of days only. There are various reasons why a given source of stress leads to different reactions in different people. For example, a person who lost a parent at an early age might perceive a current loss as more severe than someone without an early loss. However, unless someone has major depressive disorder, his or her reaction does not tend to result in a major depressive episode.

Q I've heard of a condition called dysthymia. What is it?

Dysthymia is a condition that lies somewhere between adjustment disorder with depressed mood and major depressive disorder. It is a low-grade, toned-down form of major depressive disorder. The symptoms are less numerous and less intense than those of a major depressive episode, and the condition must last for about 2 years to be considered dysthymia. In previous years, dysthymia was sometimes called chronic depression. People with dysthymia generally do not feel as bad as those with major depressive disorder. Dysthymia is not as biological in origin as major depressive disorder, and it does not respond so well to antidepressants.

Q Isn't depression genetic?

Depression does tend to run in families. There are even some detailed family tree studies showing a genetic pattern. What is inherited appears to be a vulnerability to major depressive episodes, whether the depressed person is stressed or not. Once the depressive episode is triggered, it tends to have a life of its own until treated. In any case, most doctors consider major depression and bipolar depression to be inherited conditions; other forms of biological depression might be inherited too. However, reactive depressions are not considered to be genetic. They might also run in families, but with less clear patterns. In these cases, it may be family child-rearing traditions that predispose its members to reactive depression. Remember, not everything that runs in families is genetic; poverty often runs in families, as does interest in certain careers. The genetics of depression is much more complicated than, for example, that of eye colour.

Myth "You have to feel depressed to be depressed"

Truth Even during a major depressive episode, one does not actually have to feel depressed. Feeling depressed (depressive mood) is only one of the two essential criteria used in diagnosing depression. The other essential criterion, disinterest, is sufficient for the diagnosis of a major depressive episode. That is, a person must have either depressive mood or diminished interest in things that were previously of interest to him or her. Then three or more minor criteria must be present (decreased energy; change in sleep, appetite, activity, or self-esteem; decreased concentration; or preoccupation with death).

Recognizing depression

Q How would depression affect my behaviour?

Depression can affect your behaviour in several ways. In the short-term you might seek solitude; even staying at home or in bed much of the time. Medium-term behaviour might include not pursuing opportunities because you feel "nothing is worth it". Long-term behaviour might include not finishing school, deteriorating work performance leading to dismissal, and ruining relationships, even marriage. Overall, you are likely to be less active, less motivated to pursue goals, and less interactive than usual. Most of this derives from depressive thoughts and feelings. For example: "if nothing feels good or works out, why do anything?" If everything seems so overwhelming, even seeking treatment feels impossible.

Q How would depression affect my thinking?

People with depression often have a difficult time concentrating. Even if they do not, they tend to become pessimistic. For them, the glass always appears half empty rather than half full. For example, a person who is depressed may be very miserly with money, fearing bankruptcy if it is spent – even though he or she may actually be quite affluent. Depressed people often think that they and others around them are "lesser people". They may also take the view that nothing – even attending to one's appearance – is worth it. Life appears grey, negative, boring, and the future holds little or nothing. Everything is the same, day in and day out. One common depressive refrain to the greeting, "How's it going?" is "Same as ever".

Q How can I recognize depression in someone close to me?

Generally, although not always, depression renders people less active. They might sit around all day or stay in bed. They might frown or wring their hands. People who are depressed often give less attention to appearance, so clothing, if it is even put on, won't match or fit. Much of the time, depressed people don't react to what others find interesting or funny and, quite often, they just want to be left alone. Overall, people tend to become inactive and pull back from involvement with life.

Q Is depression easy to recognize in others?

Generally, the onset of depression is difficult to recognize. This is because the depressed person tends to pull back, even hide his or her new limitations. When lack of concentration is an early symptom, adults can hide it easily. They just do not read as much, and their conversations are less involved. Adolescents tend to have a difficult time with school work, but they are well skilled in hiding this from their parents. When sleep difficulty is an early symptom, even the individual concerned might mistake the depression for everyday stress. Others will not notice the onset of depression because they are still sleeping well. Appetite decrease, especially with weight loss, is often considered a success, and a drop in self-esteem may be seen as realistic modesty. Even other symptoms, such as disinterest, changes in activity level, feeling guilty, and thinking about death tend to come on so gradually, they are hardly perceptible until some reasonable demand on the person is not met. As in most conditions, the milder cases are harder to spot. Both the individual affected and those around him or her often overlook changes or minimize their significance.

THE EFFECTS OF DEPRESSION

Depression can affect you in a variety of ways. This is a summary of its possible effects on your mind and body. If you believe that you or a member of your family is depressed, it is important to seek a proper diagnosis from a doctor. For more about the effects of depression, see pp69–109.

EFFECTS ON THOUGHTS
- You are less interested in things
- Your ability to concentrate declines
- You have more trouble making decisions
- You are less optimistic
- You are more pessimistic
- Your motivation declines
- Your self-esteem is lowered

EFFECTS ON FEELINGS
- You feel down and depressed
- You worry more
- You feel more anxious
- Your will to live is lowered (you may feel suicidal)
- You have less ability to love
- You have less ability to experience pleasure (anhedonia)
- You handle anger differently
- Your sense of hope diminishes
- Your sense of helplessness increases
- You have feelings of guilt that are not linked to anything specific

EFFECTS ON YOUR BODY
- Your sleep pattern changes
- Your appetite changes
- You gain or lose weight
- Your activity level changes
- You feel worse at a specific time of day (diurnal variation)
- You have less energy than usual
- Your interest in sex diminishes

Diagnosing depression

Q How do doctors diagnose depression?

Doctors diagnose depression by looking at a person's symptoms and signs. Symptoms are reported by the individual, whereas signs are independent observations made by others. An example of a symptom might be insomnia, whereas weeping might be an example of a sign. The pattern of symptoms and signs is used as a tool for diagnosis in all medical conditions. Although signs might be considered more objective and therefore more accurate, symptoms generally reveal what an observer cannot perceive. Some people describe their internal state very well. This can provide essential information as to whether or not they are depressed and, later, if their condition is improving. Sometimes signs and symptoms yield the same information. For example, an individual might report that he or she is feeling low (a symptom) and the doctor might notice a downcast facial expression (a sign). Both reflect the same thing – the negative emotion of depression.

Q Will a doctor take into account what my family has to say about me?

Yes. When diagnosing depression, a doctor will listen to any observations made by people who are close to you; this is called "collateral information". For example, a member of your family might report that you have become more grumpy recently, that you have lost interest in sex, or that you no longer clean your room – these are things that a doctor would not be able to observe directly. Although this information is not always as valid as a sign that can be directly witnessed by the doctor, it can still play a part in diagnosis.

Q What are the main symptoms of depression?

The symptoms that are used for diagnosing a major depressive episode (see p11) are depressive mood, diminished interest in usual activities, changes in sleep and appetite, diminished energy and activity levels, lowered self-esteem, lowered ability to concentrate, tearfulness, inability to make decisions, and thinking about death; in particular about suicide. You don't need to have all of these symptoms to be diagnosed with depression; it can be sufficient to have just some of them. The criteria for diagnosing depression come from a handbook created by the World Health Organization (WHO) called the *International Statistical Classification of Diseases and Related Health Problems, 10th revision* (known for short as *ICD-10*). The section on psychological problems in this manual was developed from reviewing the scientific literature on all psychiatric conditions and by surveying thousands of clinicians, not just doctors.

Q Are there any other symptoms of depression?

Other possible symptoms include re-arranging one's affairs, such as one's will or life insurance, despite there being no generally accepted catalyst for doing so. Losing the ability to love or take pleasure in life is another symptom, although this can occur in other conditions besides depression. Another symptom is variation in mood depending on the time of day. This is called "diurnal variation". Generally, depressed people feel worse in the morning. Social withdrawal (not wanting to be with others or being reluctant to leave the house), pessimism, loss of motivation, loss of sexual interest and pleasure, and feelings of impoverishment are other symptoms of depression.

Q Can symptoms of depression vary in severity?

Yes. Each symptom can affect a depressed person to a mild, moderate, or severe degree. If you have severe concentration problems, you might lose the ability to remember what you have read. If depressive mood is your most severe symptom, you may simply feel bad. If your sleep disruption is severe, it can lead to distress both at night and during the day. Appetite change can be severe, but generally there is little correlation between decreased appetite and weight. Some people with lowered appetite gain weight and vice versa. If you have severe loss of energy, it might be hard for you to get up and get moving, despite being motivated to do so. Severe loss of motivation can also keep you at home or in bed.

Q How do doctors assess the severity of depression?

The personal suffering of the individual is the central measure of severity. Sometimes suffering intensifies as a result of a vicious circle in which a depressed person can no longer support himself or herself financially, or sustain a relationship. As well as assessing the symptoms and signs of depression, a doctor will look at disruption to work life, social life, personal care, physical health, and family relationships. Of course, the most severe manifestation of depression is death, whether by inattention to personal safety, deterioration of another medical condition, or suicide. Sometimes, however, doctors will base their diagnosis merely on the depressive mood (the symptom complained about by the patient), and the depressive affect (the patient appearing depressed to his or her doctor). Unfortunately, this can lead to unnecessary prescriptions of antidepressant medication.

Q **Which type of depression tends to be the most severe?**

Any depression in which there is a major depressive episode (see p11). During a major depressive episode people tend to lose the ability to care about what is important to them; they often do not care about anything. However, other forms of depression, such as adjustment disorder with depressed mood, can also lead to the most severe result – suicide – even though many other measures of severity are not present.

Q **What does it mean if people say I look depressed but I don't feel it?**

It is important to realize that a person can *look* depressed but not *feel* depressed and vice versa. There can sometimes be disagreements between a doctor and patient, or between family members about this. While a doctor can deal with such disagreements, family members often cannot. This can lead to arguments between people who love each other, with one saying the person is depressed, and the other denying it.

Q **What are the signs of depression?**

Appearing generally downcast (known as "depressive affect") can be a sign of depression. This can include downward gaze, frowning, and wringing hands. Disinterest and lack of motivation can also be signs. For example, a doctor may notice that a person neglects his or her appearance or fails to take medication. A pessimistic attitude can sometimes be perceived by a doctor, especially in clinical settings where the doctor is not rushed and takes the time to talk to his or her patients. Lowered self-esteem can also be recognized by a doctor who takes the time to listen. Finally, lowered concentration can sometimes be spotted by a doctor when a usually quick-witted patient has to ask the same question several times.

Myth "All depressions pass with time"

Truth Most depressions do pass with time. These include the reactive, as well as the more biological depressions, such as major depressive disorder. However, after a person has had several depressions – usually by his or her 50s – the depression can remain chronic. It would need to be treated indefinitely, as with other chronic illnesses. If the treatment is fully successful, the person will feel and function normally. However, if the treatment is only partially successful, some depressive features will remain.

Q Is anxiety a sign of depression?

Depressed people often have visible signs of anxiety, such as frequent sighing, shifting of position, dry mouth, or lapses into unclear language. They tend to cope poorly with anxiety, often worrying about things that they wouldn't ordinarily consider a problem. However, anxiety can be caused by other conditions and can certainly be a condition in itself. This is found in panic disorder, in which the individual experiences waves or attacks of anxiety, accompanied by physical changes, such as a pounding heart (palpitations), sweatiness, trouble catching his or her breath, and tremulousness. In this case, the anxiety is more than part of the depression. It is a separate disorder, called a co-morbid disorder. It is very frequent for depressed people to have co-morbid disorders, and anxiety disorders account for most of them.

Q Can anger be a sign of depression?

Yes. Depressed people can mishandle anger. This can range from lacking a sense of anger when it would be appropriate, to displaying anger over next to nothing. Anger over trivial matters often manifests itself as irritability, and this can be very detrimental to relationships.

Q Can hopelessness be a symptom of depression?

Not only can it be, a lack of hope is one of the most severe symptoms of depression. When pessimism extends to hopelessness, the glass is not just half empty; it is completely empty. The individual loses his or her will to try to seek a cure. Even to do anything; even to go on may seem pointless. In fact, hopelessness is a strong risk factor for suicide (see pp98–103).

Causes of depression

People get depressed for a variety of reasons. Some people get depressed due to their genes, their family backgrounds, or stress. Others have a medical or psychiatric problem, or a problem with alcohol abuse, that leads them to become depressed. Finally, some people get depression for reasons that are never known.

Who gets depressed?

Q What causes a person to become depressed?

There are various suspected causes of depression, such as family history or upbringing, among others. Although these are described as "causes", it is more accurate to say that they increase a person's *vulnerability* to depression rather than directly cause it. Generally, it takes a final trigger or event for depression to emerge in a vulnerable person. This final trigger may be a stressful life event such as losing a job.

Q Is depression more frequent in some families?

Yes, genetics is considered to be a factor in depression. Family tree studies over several generations reveal that there are clusters of depressed people in some families. However, it is also important to remember that some families have specific life circumstances and methods of raising children that might predispose family members to depression. Even where there is a family history of depression, it may require some sort of stressful life event to act as a trigger for depression.

Q Do women get depressed more than men?

Yes. Many studies have shown women to have twice the frequency of depressive conditions, as compared to men. About 25 per cent of women develop a major depressive episode over the course of their lives, compared to about 12 per cent of men. In the case of seasonal affective disorder (SAD), the difference can be much greater. Some studies show that women have the condition almost 4 times as frequently as men. However, it is still not clear why women tend to get depressive conditions more often than men.

Q Are people in some cultures more prone to depression?

Studies show that most cultures in the Western world and Asia have similar frequencies of depression. However, there appears to be a difference in some cultures depending on whether their immigrant or native-born members are considered. Studies are inconclusive and, very often produce results that merely reflect the way they are conducted.

Q Does illness make people more prone to depression?

In people with various medical conditions (see pp35–36), the percentage of depression is greater than in the population in general. This may be either because depression forms a direct part of the illness or because the difficulties in coping with the illness lead to depression. In the case of hypothyroidism (a condition in which the thyroid gland does not produce sufficient thyroid hormone), for example, the signs and symptoms of depression may be part of the illness. Once the individual's thyroid hormone level returns to normal, the depression generally resolves too. Finally, just the idea of having a chronic illness, which can make most people feel down, can trigger a major depressive episode in a vulnerable person.

Q What role does alcohol play in depression?

There is a chicken-and-egg relationship between alcohol abuse and depression. Alcohol or substance abuse can increase a person's vulnerability to depression. But if someone is already depressed, he or she may drink because it temporarily allows one to feel better; this is known as "self-medication". People who self-medicate may be unaware that they have a depressive condition for which there is good medical treatment available.

Myth "If your parents were depressed, you will be, too"

Truth While some forms of depression run in families, others do not. If your parents were depressed with one of the kinds of depression that has a genetic basis, you would have a greater chance of becoming depressed than the average person. However, if your parents' depressions were not genetically influenced, you would likely have the same chance of developing depression as the average person.

Genetics and upbringing

Q Are genes the underlying cause of depression?

Most doctors agree that genes are involved in a large proportion of cases of major depressive disorder. However, the way genes influence depression is not as clear-cut as, for example, the way genes influence eye colour. As advances in gene chemistry are made, the exact contribution of genes to depression is more likely to be understood. It is also important to remember that some types of depression, such as adjustment disorder with depressed mood (see pp46–47), are not thought to be influenced by genetics.

Q How does upbringing play a role?

Although scientific data is difficult to obtain in this area, most doctors believe that family background can play a role in predisposing people to depression. Experiences such as losing a parent at an early age may contribute to depression and other psychiatric conditions. Several generations ago the loss of a parent through death was not uncommon, but today a parent may be "lost" in other ways as well: through alcohol or substance abuse, physical illness, family strife, or the parent's own depression.

Q Depression runs in my mother's family. She thinks I could be depressed. Could she be right?

Yes, she could be correct. People who have lived with depression are very sensitive to the signs of it. It is not unusual for depression to be diagnosed by a family member, even before people recognize it themselves. If your mother has noticed the signs of depression in you for 2 weeks or more, you should probably take her concerns seriously.

Gender

Q **Why do women get depressed more than men?**

As yet it is not known why women are more prone to depression than men. One theory is that men may suffer from depression just as much as women, but they are much less likely to seek help. Another theory is that female hormones are involved. On the other hand, older males with physical medical illnesses tend to get depression more than older females. As the sex hormones are playing little to no role at that age, other factors must be involved.

Q **Which kinds of depression are women most vulnerable to?**

Population statistics from several studies, carried out over many years, have found women to have about twice the chance of developing a major depressive episode than men – this is characteristic of major depressive disorder (see pp48–49). Women's vulnerability to other types of depression has not been as well studied, so it is difficult to draw firm conclusions. For obvious reasons, women are more vulnerable to postnatal depression (depression following childbirth) than men.

Q **As women are more in touch with their emotions, shouldn't they cope better and get depressed less?**

Given that women tend to be more adept at handling and expressing emotions, one would expect there to be less, not more, depression in women. One would also expect women to be better able to cope with emotionally stressful situations and be competent at processing difficult emotions such as grief. The best answer to this question is that the gender differences in depression, although real, are not well understood.

Q Could female biology account for the fact that women are more prone to depression?

There certainly are some conditions and characteristics that are linked to the sex chromosomes and the genes that they carry – family tree studies can point to them. However, the genes involved in depression are likely to be multiple, so there are no conclusions at present. The new technology of gene chemistry and gene mapping may shed more light on this subject.

Q Do the female hormones predispose women to depression?

After chromosomes and genes, the female and male hormones can be considered the next most fundamental difference between the two sexes. Although there is no conclusive evidence, female hormone levels are increased and active during pregnancy, and certain kinds of depression do occur at that time. This does suggest that female hormones may play a role in depression. Despite the correlation between female hormonal changes and the onset of a major depressive episode, there is little understanding about exactly how the two are connected.

Q Why do men, who have no female hormones, get depressed at all?

The answer might be that the male hormone is similar to its female equivalent. However, the role of the male hormone in depression is not a major focus of concern in contemporary research – cutting edge research, at present, is being carried out in other directions.

Q Why do men get depressed?

Men get depressed for all sorts of reasons, such as genetic predisposition, stress, anxiety, feelings of self-reproach, as well as worries and concerns about sex, isolation, and employment. They are 3 times more likely than women to commit suicide, particularly if they are abusing alcohol or drugs, or are separated, divorced, or widowed.

Loss and grief

Q Does bereavement lead to depression?

People who are bereaved are not their usual selves. The initial reaction to their loss is often a feeling of shock, followed by numbness and a sense of detachment. Later, they may be overwhelmed by intense feelings of sadness, guilt, or anger (see p34). They don't feel very positive, are not as active as usual, and often have depressed or sad moods. Their sleep may be disrupted, and they might even occasionally think they hear the voice or feel the presence of the lost person. However, despite all of these things, the current thinking is that bereavement is a normal reaction to significant loss; that even though it can last for months, it is not a true depression. Of course, in people who are vulnerable to depression, there is a greater likelihood that depression will develop in addition to bereavement.

Q How does grief express itself?

Grief is the emotional reaction to a significant loss. The most common of these losses is the death of a loved one. Grief is triggered by a thought or reminder of the lost person and is almost always expressed through tears. Gradually, people cry less and less, as more emotion is expressed.

Q Do grief and bereavement always follow a major loss?

It is normal and generally considered necessary to go through grief and even bereavement. There must be some emotional reaction to a significant loss. When this reaction does not occur, or when it occurs incompletely, there is often an aftermath some time later.

Q How can anniversaries trigger depression?

Anniversaries can trigger depression, but the affected person may not always be aware of this, particularly if the loss happened a long time ago. One of the aims of psychotherapy is to draw out the associations between past events and current feelings. For example, a woman might describe to a therapist how her relationship with her husband becomes stressful every summer. With the therapist's help, she might realize that it was summer when a parent died, and that this triggers a depression, which in turn negatively impacts upon her relationship.

Q How do I know if I have grieved enough?

This can be hard to know. When reminders of the deceased no longer trigger intense emotion, you may have grieved enough. A better measure, however, is how you cope at the first anniversary of the loss, and at subsequent anniversaries. It is normal to think about a lost person more at the time of an anniversary and to feel sad or angry, or whatever other feelings coloured your loss. However, when your reaction is strong, or leads to depression, you may need to grieve more.

Q Why do some people grieve better than others?

There could be many reasons for this. Some people don't grieve very well because they were raised by parents who told them that crying is a sign of weakness. Others just don't have the time or energy to grieve. An example of this might be a young mother with 3 young children, who has lost her parent. Another example might be a sibling who makes all the funeral arrangements and tends to everyone else, but takes no time for himself or herself. However, as loss is a part of life, most people learn to grieve, just as they learn other rare and often private tasks in life.

STAGES OF GRIEF

People grieve in different ways, but there are some key stages that indicate a common pathway of grief. Not everyone will encounter and pass through each stage of the list below, and many will follow a different order of stages. Those who grieve may appear to have left one stage behind, only to experience it later. Coming to terms with grief eventually leads to a resolution and re-integration.

STAGE	BEHAVIOUR
Shock	Usually the first response. May include numbness, pain, or apathy.
Denial	Refusal to acknowledge the death.
Disorganization	Unable to do the simplest of things. May feel restless, aimless, helpless, and lonely.
Anger/Guilt	Begins almost at once. Includes self-blame, irritability, or anger towards fate, God, doctors, or the deceased.
Bargaining	Acknowledgment of the loss, but tries to bargain – says, for example, "If only I could..." or "If only I had..."
Bereavement	As denial breaks down, mourning and temporary depressive mood set in. A painful and lonely stage.
Anxiety	Worry about control of feelings or of going mad. Apprehension about the future.
Restitution	Attending rituals, such as the funeral, and accepting the reality of the loss.
Resolution	Gradual acceptance of the death, and that life goes on.
Re-integration	Forging new relationships and goals. The deceased has a special place in the memory. This stage can take many months or years.

Medical illness

Q **Which medical illnesses tend to lead to depression?**

Neurological illnesses, such as stroke, epilepsy, Alzheimer's disease, and Parkinson's disease, as well as illnesses that disrupt hormone levels, such as hypothyroidism and Cushing's syndrome, can lead directly to depression. Some infections, such as HIV, are thought to cause depression directly at times. Finally, cancer can lead to depression.

Q **Isn't just the idea of having a chronic medical condition enough to cause depression?**

Yes, sometimes the idea of having a medical condition can cause depression, for example, if a person is told that he or she has tested positive for HIV. However, mostly it is the discomfort and loss of function associated with an illness that leads to depression. An example is chronic pain syndrome, which is part of a variety of medical conditions. The pain – a source of stress – can trigger any of the main types of depression: a depressive mood lasting a few days, an adjustment disorder, or a major depressive episode. The association between the illness and the depression is psychological rather than biological.

Q **How can you tell the difference between a medical condition that causes depression biologically and one that causes it psychologically?**

If the medical condition and the depression develop roughly simultaneously, and intensify and diminish in synchrony with each other, this suggests a biological link. Of course, this waxing and waning may also be psychological, as it often is with chronic pain syndrome. Other clues that depression is biological are the absence of a family history of depression, depressive symptoms that don't fit the typical profile, and late age of onset. Sometimes, a medical condition such as stroke can cause both biological and psychological depression.

Q Can medical conditions lead to other psychiatric conditions apart from depression?

Yes, medical conditions can sometimes lead to anxiety and mania. However, depression is a very common psychiatric condition that results from medical conditions. In terms of psychological reactions to a chronic medical condition, depression is far and away the main type.

Q Can psychiatric problems such as ADD lead to depression?

Yes. Recent studies have shown that ADD (attention deficit disorder) or ADHD (attention deficit hyperactivity disorder) can lead to a variety of problems in adulthood, including depression and bipolar disorder. However, around half of ADD and ADHD cases are resolved almost entirely by adulthood. The exact link between ADD/ADHD and depression is being actively studied.

Q If someone is hyperactive, isn't it hard to tell they are depressed?

It is hard to conceive that a hyperactive person can be depressed. However, even without ADD/ADHD, people with depression can be overactive and agitated. Once known as "agitated depression", psychiatrists now refer to "major depressive episode with increased activity".

Q If ADD is treated, does the depression go away?

Generally not. The depressive disorders that tend to occur more in people with ADD are separate conditions. Thus, even if the ADD is successfully treated, the depressive condition would remain and require its own treatment in addition.

Q Do people with schizophrenia have depression?

Schizophrenia is a disorder of thinking, while depression is a disorder of feeling. As schizophrenia proceeds, its victims tend to become apathetic, which can sometimes be misinterpreted as depression. The exception to this is schizoaffective disorder, in which schizophrenia is combined with true depression.

The role of stress

Q How important is stress in depression?

Stress plays a role in almost all types of depression. Even a short-lived, mild depressive mood is caused by stress. Events such as failing an examination in school, losing a job opportunity, or the breakup of a relationship hardly ever occur without some feeling of depression. However, in people with depressive conditions, the depressive reaction is broader, lasts longer, and is more intense.

Q Is there a difference between acute and chronic stress?

When a stressful event is intense, yet short-lived, the depressive reaction is generally different from when a source of stress is ongoing. People who become depressed as a result of ongoing or chronic stress have a harder time getting over their depression than people who are depressed in response to an acute source of stress. The acute stressor that provokes the most severe response is the sudden, unexpected loss of a loved one. However, although the response is severe, the depression has less fuel to keep it going because the loss is clear and finished.

Q Doesn't acute stress have an aftermath?

Yes, even acute stressors leave a wake. For example, when people die, their absence must be contended with; when a job is lost, there is financial stress to cope with. Nonetheless, this is often less of a problem than a stressor that is chronic. An example of a chronic stressor is the slow death of a loved one from cancer. Often, it is not until the ongoing source of a stress reaches its conclusion, in this case the death of the loved one, that the resolution of the depression begins.

Q Can I predict whether a stressor will cause depression?

Some people tend to get depressed in response to specific stressors. For some it is loss, for others it is assault. Some people become stressed after having surgery, perhaps because they sustained physical trauma earlier in life and experience the wound and pain of surgery as an assault.

LIFE EVENTS AND STRESS

Stress makes mental and physical demands on all of us. At a low level, it is part of our everyday lives. Sometimes, this is punctuated with a sudden, high-impact, and stressful life event, such as divorce or the death of a loved one. Often, we are prone to the negative effects of long-term stress, which grinds us down and undermines our self-confidence and self-esteem – for example, an unsatisfactory job or relationship, or worries about our children. Stressors can be rated from the very high to the low.

VERY HIGH
- Loss of job
- Death of spouse
- House move
- Divorce or separation
- Illness or injury

HIGH
- Change of job
- Death of close friend
- Pregnancy
- Retirement
- Serious family illness

MODERATE
- Trouble with boss
- Worry about friends
- Large mortgage
- Spouse stops work
- Debt problems

LOW
- Small mortgage
- Christmas
- Change in diet
- Change at work

THE ROLE OF STRESS ● 39

Q **What does it mean if I can't identify the stress that triggered my depression?**

Sometimes a stressor is difficult to pinpoint. One of the goals of psychotherapy is to understand just what triggered your depression. This means you can try to avoid such triggers in the future. If triggers are unavoidable, you can at least prepare for depression and take steps to keep it short and mild.

Q **Most people I know are stressed. Does this mean that depression is part of modern life?**

Depression is a part of modern life and, as far as is known, was always a part of life. While our modern lives are considered frenetic, there always have been life events. Untimely deaths of loved ones, illness, loss of relationships, and catastrophes such as war and natural disasters have always occurred. The disruption they cause to the underlying pace of life, whether frenetic or calm, is what is stressful. These are the kinds of stressors that tend to trigger depression.

Q **Will my depression stop if my stress does?**

This is almost always the case in reactive depressions. In major depressions, however, which are more biological, the condition can continue with a life of its own even when stress stops. In most cases, however, the intensity of the depression will taper off.

Q **The doctor told my mother her depression was fully treated. Does that mean she is immune from stress?**

Not at all. What it does mean is that she is only as vulnerable to stress as when she was not depressed. When people with treated depression react to stress, they often become demoralized, think their treatment has stopped working, and discontinue it. Thus, it is important for doctors to inform patients they will react to stress just as people who never had a depression. The treated depressive may also have occasional bad days, generally the result of unrecognized, minor stressors.

Myth "If exposed to enough stress, everyone will develop depression"

Truth With a large amount of stress, anyone may feel depressed, along with anger and other emotions. However, most people will actually recover within 2 weeks. They will come up with ways of coping, such as eliminating other stress from their lives or relying on people in their social networks for support. Even in major catastrophes, such as earthquakes, floods, or war, resulting in loss of home and family, lots of people do develop depressive conditions – but certainly not everyone.

Anxiety and depression

Q What is the role of anxiety in depression?

Depressed people are often anxious and tend to handle anxiety poorly. They often express it physically by wringing their hands or frowning. Sometimes anxiety can mask depression. For example, people may go to a doctor complaining of anxiety, then, when the anxiety is treated, they may feel depressed. These people were fighting depressive symptoms that were making them anxious.

Q Is anxiety part of depression or are they separate?

Depressed people often have two separate conditions: a depressive condition and an anxiety condition. This means that the anxiety disorder has enough signs and symptoms for it to be considered a separate condition. But anxiety can also be a part of depression.

Q Is depressive anxiety different from other kinds of anxiety?

To some extent, depressive anxiety is directed at depressive themes, such as worrying about not being able to think clearly or about how everything will turn out badly.

Q Does having anxiety prolong depression or make it worse?

Anxiety does not tend to prolong depression, but it does make it worse. Both anxiety and depression should be treated straight away. The treatments for anxiety work quickly, while those for depression take longer.

Q Do anxiety conditions lead to depression?

Post-traumatic stress disorder (PTSD), an anxiety condition, is often associated with depression; people with PTSD tend to develop depression after a while. However, whether it actually causes depression is still not known. Treatment should be directed at both conditions, generally from the beginning.

Alcohol and depression

Q **Why can't I stop my husband from drinking when he's depressed?**

It partly depends on whether your husband is abusing alcohol or is alcohol dependent. A person who abuses alcohol does so despite its negative consequences, whether at home or at work. A person who is dependent on alcohol drinks despite the negative consequences *and* despite efforts to control or stop drinking. People who are alcohol dependent also often need alcohol for physiological reasons; to prevent symptoms of alcohol withdrawal, such as shaking, seizures, or delirium. They may also develop tolerance and need to drink more to get the same effect. If your husband is alcohol dependent it will be much harder for him to stop drinking than if he simply abuses alcohol.

Q **Can drinking too much alcohol cause depression?**

There is much debate about whether alcohol causes depression or whether depression causes alcohol abuse. Currently it is accepted that depressed people tend to drink more, whether to quiet depressive feelings or to release them. At the same time it is accepted that alcohol abuse and dependence can lead to depression.

Q **Why do some people get depressed only when they drink?**

Alcohol decreases anxiety and disinhibits people. As a result, suppressed emotions are released. For some people these emotions consist of anger, for others depression.

Q **My brother says he drinks to "quiet his nerves". Is there anything wrong with this?**

Your brother is "self-medicating". This occurs when a person just doesn't feel right and discovers that alcohol diminishes that feeling, However, the positive effects of alcohol are superficial and short-lived, and the negative effects, whether physical or psychological, long-lasting.

Q My father has a history of depression and drink. He's just started drinking again after a long break, but says he is not depressed. What can I do?

Your father may well have started drinking again due to depression. People who have crossed the line into alcohol or substance abuse can recover, but they can later cross the line more easily than someone who has not. Your father may be self-medicating because he has the depressive's lack of care about what happens to him; or there might be other reasons. Urge him to seek help – if he does not respond, you might have to consult his doctor. Ultimately, you and other family members must convey to him how much his behaviour hurts or upsets you – this may prompt him to get treatment.

Q Why do I sometimes feel suicidal when I'm drunk, but not when I'm sober?

Alcohol decreases anxiety, including the anxiety that stops us from doing what we would never do when sober. Apart from disinhibiting our actions, it also allows us to *feel* what would otherwise be too frightening to feel. Other depressive symptoms can also be uncovered. When you stop drinking, your depressive symptoms, including suicidal thoughts, can be buried again. If you don't seek treatment for your underlying depression, you are likely to get into a negative cycle of behaviour.

Q When I stopped drinking, I felt depressed. My doctor wanted me to take an antidepressant, but my AA sponsor said to wait. What should I do?

Chronic drinking can lead to depression but depression can also lead to alcohol abuse. The challenge is to tell which came first. If your alcohol abuse is relatively chronic, it's likely that it is causing the depression. As you stop drinking, the depression will emerge and subside over time. About 1 or 2 months are considered enough time to tell if the depression is due to alcohol or has a life of its own. If depression is independent of alcohol abuse, it should be treated – but Alcoholics Anonymous (AA) meetings should also continue.

Types of depression

Although the various different types of depression tend to share symptoms and come and go in episodes, they have different causes and triggers. Depressive episodes also last for differing amounts of time, and some types of depression are more likely to recur than others. The treatment your doctor offers you will depend on the type of depression you have.

Reactive depression

Q What is reactive depression?

This is a type of depression that happens in response to a specific, identifiable source of stress in your life (a stressor). This stress could arise from many sources: from problems in your relationship with your partner, child, or other family members to financial or work problems. See p38 for a description of common stressors and to what degree they might have an impact on you. Reactive depression is also known as adjustment disorder.

Q After my husband left me, I felt low and couldn't sleep or eat for days. My doctor said I had a reactive depression. How long will it last?

Considering that your stressor – the separation from your husband – is clear to you and you have only the symptoms you listed, you probably have an adjustment disorder with depressed mood. Adjustment disorders last less than 6 months after the stressor ends. If your symptoms persist longer or become stronger, you have a different type of depression.

Q When I lost my job, I got nervous as well as depressed. Can reactive depression give me anxiety?

Yes, although there is a slightly different name for this: adjustment disorder with mixed emotions. Loss of a job is a severe enough stressor to bring on a reactive depression, with or without anxiety. However, as a job loss is final, your reaction will generally resolve quickly.

Q How severe can reactive depression be?

Immediately after you experience the stressor that is triggering your depression, your reaction can be severe, even to the point of suicide. However, symptoms usually calm down in a few days and continue until the stress is overcome. In the case of a job loss, getting a new job will generally lead to a lifting of the depression.

Q **I couldn't stop crying after my wife died. My doctor suggested an antidepressant. Was that necessary?**

It sounds like you were grieving, which is not considered a depression at all; an antidepressant medication would have no effect. Your grief is likely to turn into a state of bereavement, in which you might feel a bit depressed but, unless this lasts for months, it is a normal state. Perhaps you looked depressed to your doctor or, if you have had a true depression in the past, perhaps your doctor may have wanted to prevent another episode.

Q **Can reactive depression be treated?**

Reactive depressions generally have few symptoms, and these can be treated. If your sleep is disrupted, a sleeping pill or deep relaxation can help. If you are not eating, a high calorie supplement can help keep your weight and energy up. Psychotherapy can help you sort out your feelings, especially about the stressor that triggered your depression. You may also be prescribed an antidepressant. Modern antidepressants are very mild compared to their predecessors, so you and your doctor might feel they are worth a try, especially if your symptoms are close to those of a major depressive episode. Simple strategies, such as avoiding extra stress at work and at home, can also help.

Q **Is my reactive depression likely to recur?**

This depends largely on the stressor involved. For example, if it was the loss of your last parent, you can't lose another. However, if you were depressed by the loss of a relationship, this can happen again. You may be able to change how you respond to a stressor with psychotherapy. For example, if you grew up very poor, the loss of a job might affect you more than someone from a wealthy background. With a therapist's help, you might learn to accept that you have more skills than your parents and won't end up poor just because they did.

Major depressive disorder

Q What is major depressive disorder?

It is a condition in which you have one or more major depressive episodes, but never a manic one. People with major depressive disorder are biologically predisposed to depression, although individual depressive episodes may be triggered by stress. The lay term "clinical depression" is sometimes used to describe this disorder, but it is not used by physicians or in psychiatric literature.

Q My depression came on gradually and nothing specific seemed to trigger it. Have I got major depressive disorder?

Major depressive episodes often start in this way. If you have the usual symptoms and signs (see pp15–23), you are likely to have the disorder. Some depressive episodes don't have an identifiable stressor. Others have one, but it could be mild and you may come to recognize it only with the help of a psychotherapist. Major depressive disorder is considered biological in nature because often there is no clear stressor, or the effect of the stressor is negligible.

Q How long do major depressive episodes last?

Major depressive episodes have to last at least 2 weeks. They can persist for months or years. Each one is often longer and stronger without treatment. After several recurrences, they may become permanent (chronic). To tell if the depression has become chronic, the medication is tapered off slowly and the doctor's appointments are made more frequent, to catch recurrence of depressive symptoms and signs. If some re-emerge, the medication is increased back to its previous level. A few months later, this is repeated.

Q Do major depressive episodes recur?

Almost by definition, major depressive episodes recur. Only occasionally does a person get just one. The recurrences tend not to be time related, for example every 5 years, but they can be. Generally, they recur after the reappearance of a particular stressor for a given person, as if this stressor were a psychological "Achilles' heel". Often, though, no stressor is apparent.

Q Do I need to take medication for a major depressive episode?

Many people do, because, if left untreated, the episode tends to be worse in terms of severity and duration. You might be prescribed an antidepressant for your depressive symptoms and signs, a sleep medication for sleep problems, and an anti-anxiety medication (known as an "anxiolytic") if you are experiencing anxiety. If effective, medication can cut short a depression that could otherwise significantly disrupt your life. Once the antidepressant medication begins to work, the anxiolytic and sleep medication can often be stopped.

Q I'm seeing a psychologist for my depression. Is this appropriate if I have a major depressive disorder?

Major depressive disorder can be treated by both psychotherapy and medication, so there is no need to stop seeing your psychologist, especially if you have built up a good relationship with him or her. You can ask your doctor to prescribe medication or refer you to a psychiatrist who can prescribe it. However, it is very important for your psychologist (or any other therapist) and the prescribing doctor to communicate, so each knows what is going on in your treatment. If your depression worsens, the best person to prescribe medication would be a psychiatrist, who is likely to see you at fairly frequent intervals. Even if you are seeing a psychiatrist, you can still continue to have psychotherapy.

Bipolar disorder

Q What is bipolar disorder?

Bipolar disorder is a type of depression characterized by major depressive episodes, manic episodes, and mixed episodes. Because manic episodes are almost entirely different from depressive episodes, they are referred to as "poles", as in the North and South Poles.

Q What's the difference between having bipolar disorder and being manic-depressive?

Essentially none. These two terms generally refer to the same condition. For almost a century, the term manic-depressive illness or manic-depressive disease was used to describe the condition. However, the current term is bipolar disorder.

Q Are there different types of bipolar disorder?

Bipolar disorder includes a range of mood-swing conditions of varying severity. The most severe among these is Bipolar Type I, which requires hospitalization for the manic phase of the condition. More moderate forms are Bipolar Type II, which doesn't require hospitalization, and cyclothymia, which involves very frequent, but much milder changes in mood. Within each type of bipolar disorder, in mania, moods can swing from elevated to depressed in an instant.

Q Is the depressed phase of bipolar disorder any different from a regular depression?

No, the depressed phase of bipolar disorder (called "bipolar depressed") is the same as a major depressive episode. In fact, there are cases in which a person has repeated major depressive episodes and is diagnosed as having major depressive disorder. Then later in life, he or she finally has a manic episode – in retrospect the correct diagnosis should have been bipolar disorder.

Q **How is a manic episode different from a major depressive one?**

The symptoms and signs of a major depressive episode are almost always opposite to those of a manic one. While some aspects of the manic episodes may appear positive, they are often ruinous because they are excessive.

DIFFERENCES BETWEEN DEPRESSION AND MANIA

SIGNS/SYMPTOMS OF DEPRESSION	SIGNS/SYMPTOMS OF MANIA
• Depressed mood	• Elated mood or agitation
• Disinterest in or boredom with usual pursuits	• Exaggerated interest in usual pursuits and/or in additional pursuits
• Interrupted sleep	• No need for sleep
• Low energy (anergia) and low activity	• High energy (hyperenergetic), overactivity
• Low self-esteem	• Elevated self-esteem, overconfidence
• Diminished concentration	• Sense of increased concentration
• Pre-occupation with death	• Feeling enlivened
• Feelings of hopelessness, pessimism	• Feelings of hope, confidence, optimism
• Lack of motivation	• Excessive motivation
• Flat/depressed affect	• Labile (changeable) affect, mood swings
• Tendency to be socially withdrawn	• Seemingly socially engaged, charismatic
• Sense of impoverishment	• Sense of plenty, spending sprees
• Repetitive/obsessive thinking	• Tangential thinking
• If psychotic, deprecating themes	• If psychotic, grandiose themes
• Loss of pleasure (anhedonia)	• Pleasure, even overindulgence
• Rarely laughing	• Easily laughing, joking

Q **What is a mixed episode?**

A bipolar mixed episode is one in which the diagnostic criteria for both a major depressive episode and a manic episode are met nearly every day for at least a week.

Q **How long does each phase of manic depression generally last?**

A bipolar depressed episode usually lasts as long as any other major depressive episode. A manic episode, however, is usually shorter, perhaps weeks to months. In about half the cases of manic episodes, a major depressive episode occurs immediately before or afterward.

Q **Does bipolar depression keep coming back?**

Bipolar episodes, whether depressive or manic, recur. Classically, it was said that the recurrences came at regular intervals for a given person, for example once every 2 years. It is now recognized that recurrence intervals vary considerably, even in the same patient.

Q **My uncle has bipolar disorder. Why wasn't he simply given an antidepressant when he was depressed?**

The problem with an antidepressant is that it will lift a person with bipolar disorder back to a normal level, but then it can continue lifting them to the level of mania, at which point harmful and dangerous behaviour can occur. For many years, this problem was tackled by using both an antidepressant and a medication called a mood stabilizer.

Q **Why was I prescribed a mood stabilizer but not an antidepressant for my bipolar disorder?**

In recent years, studies have shown that using a mood stabilizer by itself can return a bipolar depressed person to his or her normal self. Sometimes a mood stabilizer is given a chance to work by itself – if it doesn't, an antidepressant is added. However, some doctors opt for an antidepressant straight away, because it takes 2 weeks to start working. If the mood stabilizer works, the antidepressant can be stopped.

Pre- and postnatal depression

Q What do pre- and postnatal depressions mean?

Pre- and postnatal depressions are sub-types of major depressive disorder. They affect women during pregnancy or in the period after childbirth and share the symptoms of major depressive disorder (see pp19).

Q Doesn't everyone get the "baby blues"?

"Baby blues" is a term for the mild form of depression that many, if not most, women get after childbirth. Its symptoms and signs are not severe, and the ability to function on a day-to-day level is minimally compromised. "Baby blues" usually last for 2 or 3 months after childbirth. On the other hand, postnatal depression is characterized by more severe and prolonged signs and symptoms and, in some cases, by psychosis.

Q My daughter was depressed during her pregnancy. Why wasn't she prescribed medication?

Treating depression during pregnancy, as with all medical conditions during this time, requires consideration of the unborn child. Studies show that some medications are more likely than others to cause defects in the unborn child. As always, every treatment decision comes down to a risk-benefit analysis. For example, if a woman is so depressed that she is not taking care of herself or her baby, or is significantly suicidal, then the risk of potential damage to the baby through treatment may be justified in order to protect the life of both mother and baby. However, most cases are not so clear-cut and doctors are often faced with clinical dilemmas.

Q Are there any non-drug treatments that can be used during pregnancy?

Yes, both psychotherapy and electroconvulsive therapy (ECT) can be used without harm to the unborn child. Psychotherapy can enable the mother to work on issues that relate to having a child. A psychotherapist can also monitor the severity of depression and suggest additional treatment if necessary. ECT is usually reserved for severe cases or ones in which antidepressants cannot be taken.

Q Does depression during pregnancy go away after the child is born?

Sometimes but not always. If it does continue after childbirth, the mother can start antidepressant treatment in the postnatal period, although this does mean that she would need to stop breastfeeding because the medication can be passed to the baby via breast milk.

Q What causes postnatal depression?

Much research has been focused on the rapid hormonal shifts that take place after pregnancy. However, as yet there is no consensus about the role of hormones.

Q My daughter has postnatal depression and won't take care of her baby. What can I do?

Beyond routine childcare, there are two things that are very important. The first is to protect the infant. Some mothers with postnatal depression neglect their babies or even harm them. The second thing is to encourage your daughter to get treatment for her depression.

Q What happens if postnatal depression is not treated?

Postnatal depression can last for years. The acute symptoms generally stabilize into a more chronic, insidious form, and outsiders may not notice that anything is wrong. During this time, there is often disinterest and neglect of the child, and a lack of bonding, nurturing interactions between mother and child. In severe cases, especially if psychosis develops, mothers have been known to seriously harm their children.

Q **I had postnatal depression after my delivery. Will it happen again in the future?**

You do have a substantially increased risk of postnatal depression with each pregnancy – the major risk factor for postnatal depression is a previous episode. Many women who have had this type of depression are faced with difficult family planning decisions.

RISK FACTORS FOR POSTNATAL DEPRESSION

RISK FACTOR	COURSE OF ACTION
Previous postnatal depression	• Early treatment • Adoption • Limit family size
Previous major depressive episode	• Take time to work on best and fastest treatment for you
Family history of major depression	• Let your doctor know • Ask family members what worked for them • Pre-natal psychiatric consultation
Depression and anxiety during pregnancy	• Pre-natal consultation • Close postnatal monitoring
Stress during pregnancy	• Psychotherapy
Low social support	• Build social network prenatally
Poor marital adjustment	• Couples therapy • Family involvement
Cigarette smoking	• Education on negative effects on fetus • Family involvement
Formula feeding exclusively	• Early monitoring • Exploration of aversion to breastfeeding

Myth "Depression after pregnancy is expected and mild"

Truth Although depression is very common after pregnancy, it is not always mild. Depression must be taken seriously, as it can be so severe that the infant is neglected or even harmed by the mother – such is the power of depression. In such cases of true postnatal depression, a recurrence is, in fact, expected with each pregnancy. This is why couples so affected must face difficult family planning decisions, such as adoption.

Premenstrual depression

Q I feel very low before my period. Is this normal PMS?

Generally, premenstrual syndrome (PMS) refers to bothersome, but not severe, anxiety and tension before menstruation, which disappears as menstruation begins. However, some women have more severe symptoms and signs that include anxiety, mood swings, tearfulness, and irritability, which may impact negatively on relationships. The symptoms and signs may resemble those of major depressive disorder but they do not last as long – as with PMS, they end as menstruation starts. This condition is sometimes referred to as premenstrual dysphoric disorder.

Q How is premenstrual depression treated?

Medical treatment alleviates symptoms rather than addressing the underlying cause. If anxiety is your main symptom, you may be prescribed an anxiolytic; if it is depressed mood, you may be given an antidepressant. Antidepressants can be taken throughout your cycle or just during the premenstrual stage – both are beneficial. The most beneficial antidepressants appear to be the selective serotonin reuptake inhibitors (SSRIs; see pp153–159).

Q I've heard that testosterone may treat premenstrual symptoms. How does it work?

It would not be surprising if some hormone problem were at the bottom of all premenstrual symptoms, which are not just limited to depression or anxiety. Birth control pills, which alter female hormones, have also been used to alter other hormones, even the small amount of testosterone women have. One might think that bringing testosterone to different levels would work to relieve PMS. However, no experiments to date have shown this.

Illness-related depression

Q How can I tell if my depression is the result of an underlying medical illness?

It can be difficult to tell sometimes. Some medical conditions, such as hypothyroidism, are so commonly involved in depression that they are routinely tested for. In some other cases, depression may be caused by a brain tumour, and this is less easy to identify because brain scans are not routinely done unless some of the physical symptoms or signs of a brain tumour are present.

Q I took strong pain medications for my back problem and then became depressed. Could the two be connected?

Actually, all *three* could be connected. Firstly, chronic pain can lead to depression. Secondly, depression can sustain chronic pain. Thirdly, strong pain medication, which generally means narcotic medication such as morphine or oxycodone, can lead to many of the symptoms of depression. If your depressive symptoms are attributable to pain medication, the aim of modern pain management is to lower your dose to the point at which the depressive symptoms lift. Although a lower dose may mean that you experience some pain, it is likely that you will still be able to function better than if you were depressed.

Q Are there any other drugs that can cause depression?

Yes, depression can be a side effect of both prescription and illicit drugs. These range from prescription oxycodone to the illicit heroin. Cortisone is a prescription drug (used to treat autoimmune and other diseases) that can cause both depression and mania. Some medications for high blood pressure, such as alpha methyldopa and reserpine, also cause depression, but they are no longer used. Birth control pills can cause depression, as can some cardiac medications and muscle relaxants.

Q How would I know if drugs were responsible for my depression?

If you have never been depressed before and your depression coincides with the use of a new drug, particularly one that is implicated in depression, such as cortisone, there may well be a link between the two. If you cannot stop using the drug, you will need to be treated for depression, as well as the underlying medical condition.

Q If my depression is related to an illness, which should be treated first?

In general, if the medical condition can be treated easily and quickly, as is the case with hypothyroidism, and the depression is not severe, treatment of the underlying medical condition can begin first. On the other hand, if the medical condition is largely untreatable, such as stroke, antidepressant treatment can start straight away. In cases that fall in the middle of this spectrum, such as Parkinson's disease, most doctors would treat both from the beginning. All doctors involved in prescribing medication need to communicate and share information about how the underlying condition and the depression are responding. Any interactions between drugs also need to be monitored.

Q After I had a heart attack, the doctors said my test results were fine, but I couldn't get back to normal. Finally, my doctor said I was depressed. Could this have been picked up earlier?

Simply put, yes. More and more studies demonstrate that a high percentage of depression is linked to medical illnesses. This is a public health problem that may be best approached with awareness and education. Sometimes, patients fill in questionnaires to rate whether they are depressed, but results can be confusing because depression may be mild at first, and because people cannot decide if their symptoms are due to physical illness or depression. In the future, it is likely that doctors will ask patients about symptoms of depression. However, despite the growing awareness about illness and depression, patients may be reluctant to report these symptoms to a doctor.

Psychotic depression

Q What is psychosis?

Psychosis involves losing touch with reality. People who have psychoses can have hallucinations, such as hearing voices that are not present. They may also have delusions – believing things that are not possible. An example of a psychotic delusion would be the belief that one's thoughts are being broadcast so that others can witness them. Another delusion might be that the television, radio, moon, or stars are somehow sending a message specifically to the individual (this type of delusion is called an idea of reference). Psychotic depression refers to a major depressive episode combined with psychosis. Psychosis makes a major depressive episode worse.

Q What makes someone have a psychotic depression rather than an ordinary depression?

It is still unknown just what predisposes a person with depression to develop psychosis with it. There are some conditions in which brief episodes of psychosis occur under stress, with or without depression. It is not surprising, then, that people with these conditions will, when developing a depression, have psychosis, too.

Q My sister is depressed and she says she will be punished by Satan. Is this a sign of psychosis?

You would need to ask her specific questions to find out what her true thoughts are. If she really believes what she is saying, she would be diagnosed as having a psychosis. If her depression and her psychosis are related, the psychosis is referred to as mood-congruent. This means that her psychotic thoughts are related to her depressive mood: she thinks she is bad and will be punished. People with depression often feel guilty, although what they feel guilty about is not always clear.

Q If I have one psychotic depression, will I have another?

There is no recognized tendency to repeat psychosis when a depression recurs. One may or may not develop psychosis with each depression. Nevertheless, psychosis generally makes any depression so much worse that it must be looked for very carefully.

Q Is psychosis part of postnatal depression?

It can be. Psychosis is generally diagnosed in new mothers who kill their babies. Such cases are very rare but they receive a great deal of media attention. This can lead people to the misconception that all women with postnatal depression are at risk of killing their children. When women do kill their children, it is usually because they believe that the children are better off dead – they are often responding to instructions from God or Satan. A tragic aspect of this is the fact that postnatal depression with psychosis is treatable.

Q How does psychosis worsen depression?

One way is that psychosis can take the form of auditory hallucinations, which is hearing what is not present. When the hallucinations are commanding in nature (they tell a person what to do), and when the command is to harm himself or herself, the person must constantly struggle not to do so. This can be exhausting, and when unsuccessful, can lead to suicide. Another psychotic variant is paranoia. People with paranoia may believe even their loved ones are conspiring against them. Yet another problem is subtle psychosis. Because it is subtle, it is often not recognized as psychosis. Rather, its effects are more insidious and not considered part of an illness. The individual may make paranoid accusations that are taken at face value, and much effort must be expended defending them. Once the psychosis stops, the accusations stop.

Q **Do schizophrenia and depression tend to occur together?**

People with schizophrenia (a chronic disease characterized by psychosis) can also develop the type of depression that meets the criteria for a major depressive episode. This is known as schizoaffective disorder. For a person to receive this diagnosis, psychotic signs and symptoms of schizophrenia need to be present for at least 6 months before the depressive signs and symptoms emerge. The disorder is treated with an antipsychotic medication for the psychosis and with antidepressant medication (with or without psychotherapy) for the depression. Sometimes, people with schizophrenia develop a blandness in their delivery and presentation over time – this should not be confused with true depression.

Q **What is the difference between depression with psychosis and psychosis with depression?**

Although the treatment is essentially the same for both, the prognosis is different. People who have psychosis followed by depression are chronically affected, whereas people with depression followed by psychosis are likely to get better. Treatment for the former is designed to minimize deterioration in function, to lessen the chance of hospitalization, and to help people retain their jobs. Treatment for the latter is designed to resolve the psychosis and depression entirely – even if there are future episodes, people can live a functional life in between.

Q **Can't someone with psychotic depression be treated just for the depression?**

If depression is the primary problem, it is possible to make it the sole focus of treatment. However, psychosis can be very disturbing to people and can lead to impaired judgment, and even suicide. Also, antidepressants take a minimum of 2 weeks to work, whereas antipsychotic medication can take effect in a few days. For these reasons, treatment for both problems usually starts straight away.

Seasonal affective disorder

Q **What is seasonal affective disorder (SAD) and who is likely to get it?**

This is a seasonal type of depression that occurs during times of the year when there are low levels of sunlight. The signs and symptoms are the same as those of a major depressive episode, even though they may be very mild. These symptoms then tend to resolve in spring as the days grow lighter. Young people are more prone to SAD, and women are more vulnerable than men.

Q **How can I treat SAD? Is light therapy effective?**

Light therapy involves sitting close to a special lamp (the wavelength of the light is important) for about 2 hours a day, at a specific time of day. If successful, this starts to work in about 2 weeks. Many people find this regimen too constraining and switch to antidepressants. Melatonin (a chemical related to the sleep-wake cycle) has also been used for treating SAD, but has proved ineffective.

SEASONAL AFFECTIVE DISORDER AND ITS TREATMENT

DESCRIPTION	Depression begins in autumn or winter, and lifts in spring.
RISK FACTORS	• **Higher latitudes** Regions where there is less light in autumn/winter in contrast to spring/summer • **Age** More prevalent in youth; often resolves with age • **Sex** More prevalent in women
TREATMENT	• **Light therapy** Sitting near to a special light for an hour or two at same time each day • **Vacations** Time spent in regions of lower latitude provides more exposure to sunlight • **Medications** Antidepressants are an option for people who tire of light therapy

Depression in childhood

Q Can children get depressed in the same way as adults?

Depression can occur in childhood and adolescence but it may reveal itself differently from the way it reveals itself in adulthood. Children and adolescents may first show signs of depression by being more sensitive, snappy, or irritable than usual. Depression may come on slowly and gradually, which is why it may be spotted more easily by someone outside your immediate family who is not in close day-to-day contact with your child. Teachers may not detect depression because children often withhold their feelings in class. Changed behaviour or a change in your child's personality can be a sign of depression, since depression is a condition superimposed on a person's normal self.

Q My son has become become very lazy recently. Could he be depressed?

If laziness marks a change in your son, it could well be a sign of depression. However, if laziness is part of his make-up, and there are no other signs or symptoms of depression, then depression is unlikely. In depressed children, laziness or being "a couch potato" is often the first change that parents complain about.

Q I have bipolar disorder in my family. Can my depressed son become bipolar?

Yes, even children and adolescents can get bipolar disorder. The development of uncharacteristic, outrageous, or risky behaviour in a child may be an initial sign of bipolar disorder. If antidepressants are prescribed for a bipolar depressed child, a mood stabilizer may also be given to prevent a manic switch from depression. As with adults, a mood stabilizer alone may be enough.

Q Our doctor
recommended
we take our 13-
year-old son to a
psychiatrist. Is this
really necessary?

It depends on what is happening to your son. Children
and adolescents often try to hide their problems, both
from you and from themselves. It takes special skill to get
a child or adolescent to open up and reveal what is going
wrong – this is where a psychiatrist who is trained in
communicating with young people can be of great help.

Q What happens if
I don't take our
teenager to
a psychiatrist?

Depression goes away with time in children and
adolescents, just as it does with adults. However, if
the symptoms are painful for your child, you might
not want to wait for things to get better. There is also
the possibility that things may get worse: additional
problems include a deterioration in schoolwork, alcohol
and drug abuse, loss of friends, trouble with the law,
and/or suicide.

Q Can psychotherapy
alone cure my child's
depression?

The treatment that yields the best results for depression
in childhood is a combination of psychotherapy and
antidepressant medication. However, psychotherapy
alone can still help, especially if the depression is mild or
moderate. Interpersonal psychotherapy (see p142–143)
has been shown to help adolescents. It is designed to be
relatively short-term and to focus on relationships.

Q Is it true that
antidepressants
can actually cause
suicide in children?

Recent studies have shown that in some cases,
suicidality is increased by antidepressant use in
adolescents. Suicidality is defined in this context as
thinking about suicide or making a suicide attempt.
So far, there have been no cases of actual suicide due
to antidepressant use, but, with time, there may
well be. If children are given antidepressants, they
should be watched for risk factors for suicide.

Depression in old age

Q My 80-year-old uncle is frail and lives alone. Wouldn't he be depressed?

You have accurately defined some of the risk factors for depression. It is definitely stressful to be in one's 80s – one is closer to death than at 40, and it is also more difficult to remain active and to control one's environment. Men also become more prone to depression with age. Finally, isolation is a major stressor that can lead to depression. Despite all this, your uncle does not *have* to be depressed. There are ways to deal with his risk factors.

Q Ever since my father started to lose his faculties, he seems depressed. Can anything be done?

If your father's faculties are slipping, he may well have some sort of dementia. The most common types of dementia are Alzheimer's dementia, in which memory deteriorates due to degeneration of brain tissues, and vascular dementia (this used to be called multi-infarct dementia). Vascular dementia occurs when small blood vessels in the brain get blocked, damaging parts of the brain that are served by those vessels. The condition deteriorates in a gradual, step-like fashion, as progressively more and more blood vessels become blocked. Both Alzheimer's dementia and vascular dementia can lead to depression, but it often goes unrecognized because the signs and symptoms may be attributed to dementia. Antidepressants and psychotherapy can often help considerably in such cases. Sometimes, a deterioration in mental function is not due to dementia at all, although it appears to be. This is called pseudodementia, and it is reversible with antidepressant treatment.

Q **My mother is given a lot of medication by her nursing home. Could it be making her depressed?**

Taking specific pain medications and sedatives can lead to depression – if this is the case, it is important for your mother's doctor to review the relevant medications and to try to change them where possible. Sometimes a significant symptom of depression is disturbance to sleep. In nursing homes, this may be dealt with by prescribing more sleeping medication – as a result, the affected person sleeps better, but the symptom of depression gets masked. If you think this is happening, a polite but assertive approach often works.

Q **My grandfather is depressed, but he doesn't want medication for it. Are there other things he can try?**

The choice is broad, so any starting point depends on his particular situation. If he is isolated, encourage him to socialize. Doing voluntary work can also help him. If he is taking other medication, ask his doctor to review it. If your grandfather has an underlying medical condition, ask his doctor about that too. If the condition is treatable, even partially treatable, then the depression could resolve too.

Q **What issues should I be aware of now that my elderly mother is taking antidepressants?**

The general guideline for doctors when they treat the elderly is: "start low and go slow". This refers to the raising of the dose until the treatment works. The elderly often take more time to adjust to new medications and any side effects may affect them more. Taking antidepressants can affect the body's ability to clear itself of other medications. This can mean that if your mother is taking other medications – which is likely due to her age – they may build up to an unacceptable level in her body. All of your mother's doctors need to know which medications she is taking so that they can adjust the prescriptions as necessary.

Effects of depression

Depression affects both your mind and your body. It can disturb your ability to concentrate and make decisions; it can also have a negative impact on your appetite, sleep, energy levels, and sexual desire. In time, the effects of depression on your mind and body translate into changes in your behaviour and social interactions.

Concentration and memory

Q Can depression affect my ability to think?

Yes, depression can diminish your ability to concentrate, which means it takes more mental effort to think about even the simplest of daily activities. If your depression belongs to the type that includes psychotic symptoms and signs, your thinking will become even more disrupted. Elderly people with depression sometimes have so much difficulty thinking that they appear to have dementia (pseudodementia). However, concentration problems are reversible and generally go away as your depression lifts.

Q I'm struggling to remember the things I read. Is memory loss part of depression?

It is more likely that you are losing your ability to concentrate. Loss in concentration and memory can be easily confused, but their differences are quite important. Memory loss is usually permanent, and is a characteristic of neurological conditions. Loss of concentration is generally temporary, and is found in depressive conditions.

Q How can I tell whether my problems are related to memory or concentration?

If you walk into a room and forget why you went there, more often than not, you are suffering from decreased concentration. Some other examples of concentration problems are: having trouble in absorbing what you read and difficulty in following conversations, especially those in groups. On the other hand, examples of memory problems include not remembering what you had for breakfast, not remembering what you just said, and not knowing the date.

Q How can I test my concentration?

You can try some simple tests doctors use on patients. One is to say the months of the year backward. Another is to count backward from 100 by divisions of 7. Yet another is to spell words backward. In most psychiatric evaluations, a person is asked to spell the word "world" backward. These simple tests are a good measure of concentration, although it is unclear why this should be the case.

Q I think my 70-year-old father has both concentration and memory problems. Is that possible?

Yes, your father could have a neurological, as well as a psychiatric condition underlying his memory and concentration problems. However, differentiating between the two can be difficult. His doctor would need to analyse all aspects of both conditions.

Q I'm having trouble focusing at work and at home. Could I be depressed?

You could be, since depression can diminish one's ability to concentrate. Some people just cannot coordinate their thoughts, whether to answer a question or to plan things. Friends and family members might view you as inattentive or slow, and someone you do not know might even doubt your intelligence. The problem, however, is not your intelligence, but the fact that your thoughts are slowed down. This means it takes you longer and requires more effort to respond or to reach a conclusion.

Q I cannot multi-task when I'm depressed. Is that normal?

Yes, this is another example of a concentration problem. When you are depressed, it becomes more difficult to keep as much in your mind as before. People whose jobs require handling multiple bits of information simultaneously, or parents who have to juggle their children's schedules besides their own are particularly badly affected. Most people don't realize how much information they process until they lose this ability.

Decision-making

Q Could my indecisiveness be a symptom of depression?

If you were decisive earlier but are unable to make decisions now, this change may be a symptom of depression. The characteristics of depressive indecisiveness include going along with others when they disagree with you, feeling guilty about standing up for your decisions, and thinking that your decisions won't work out. Sometimes, this indecisiveness can be so severe that you may change your mind back and forth many times and struggle to get anything done at all – you become mentally paralysed. However, indecision alone doesn't mean depression. If you have other signs or symptoms, such as changes in your sleep, appetite, or energy levels, the picture would be more clear.

Q Why should depression make decision-making more difficult?

This is partly because depression involves diminished concentration, which makes focusing on a decision more difficult. In addition, making a decision requires a certain amount of self-confidence and optimism. Since both of these can also diminish in depression, it becomes more difficult to believe that your decisions will bring about positive results.

Q I've lost the sense of direction I used to have. Is this part of depression?

Although there could be many reasons why you have lost your sense of direction, depression is certainly one of them. You may have lost your ability to make decisions, and because of this, it has become more difficult for you to sift out one direction from many options. Even when it comes to going out, you may struggle to decide what to do or where to go.

Q If I keep changing my answers to test questions at school, could I be depressed?

This type of indecisiveness could be a result of depression. Depression often occurs in school-age children. If you were once able to choose an easily, but struggle to do so now, you need to talk to your parents about this.

Q My colleague lost his father this time last year. Recently he's been struggling to solve problems. Could the two be connected?

Losing a close relative can trigger depression in some people, so your colleague's loss, combined with his change in behaviour, does make depression a possibility. Solving problems and coming up with new solutions involves making many decisions. This in turn takes optimism, high self-esteem, persistence, and a desire to build rather than to let go – all of these things are diminished in depression.

Q When I'm depressed I can make simple decisions but not complex ones. Why?

Decision-making, like almost every other sign and symptom in medicine, exists on a scale that ranges from mild to severe. If your depression does not stabilize at this point, and becomes worse, you might start to experience difficulty even with simple decisions.

Q Is indecisiveness always a sign of depression?

No. There are several reasons why people struggle to make decisions – depression is just one of them. Also, there are some areas of life that depressed people often simply don't care about. If someone is struggling to decide between one relationship and another, he or she is unlikely to be depressed. This is because people with depression rarely go out and develop social contacts or pursue relationships. They don't have the necessary optimism, hope, and desire for social interaction. In fact, very often relationships tend to disintegrate in depression.

Thoughts and attitudes

Q Why does nothing seem to change in my life when I'm depressed?

You could be experiencing the sense of sameness that people with depression often have. There is a loss of pleasure and interest in life (anhedonia), so nothing feels exciting and nothing seems to matter – every day feels the same. When people ask how you are, your habitual refrain might be, "Same as ever", or words to that effect.

Q My wife has started criticizing me all the time. Is this a sign of depression?

There could be many reasons for your wife's criticisms. However, if some of the other aspects of depression are developing, then she may be depressed. People who are depressed generally become pessimistic and see the world negatively. Since you are a big part of your wife's world, she could be seeing you as negatively as everything else.

Q Why won't my husband go out when he is depressed? He just wants to sit at home and vegetate.

People with depression often don't see any reason to do things, especially things that others find pleasurable. This is because they often don't experience pleasure. Of course, there are degrees of this. Your husband might not enjoy going out, but gets pleasure from other things. The fact that you use the word "vegetate" implies that he doesn't do much at home either. He could also be manifesting the depressive's tendency to isolate himself.

Q My mother used to be very positive, but now she says "no" to everything I offer her. Why?

Your mother may be experiencing the depressive attitude of sameness. If you offer her help, she could be saying "no" because she is pessimistic and doesn't believe that anything will make a difference to the way she feels. She could also be anhedonic; if she cannot experience pleasure, whatever you offer her may seem worthless.

Q My father rarely laughs. Could he be depressed?

Laughter is an expression of pleasure and, it is possible that your father is unable to feel pleasure due to depression, which can lead to the attitude: "What's so funny?" In your father's case, it seems the depression may have become chronic, which is why you and others around him may have come to see his inability to laugh as a part of his personality.

Q Why do I just go along with things when I'm depressed?

People who are depressed tend to avoid contention. Some of them have even been known to pay bills they know they don't owe, simply to avoid a feeling of discomfort. You might be avoiding the anger or assertiveness involved in challenging something or someone you disagree with, you might be too pessimistic to think you could win, or you might just have stopped caring.

Q Why do I see the worst in people when I'm depressed?

This is quite common in depression. When you have a depressive attitude you tend to see negative or self-aggrandizing qualities in people. For example, if a parent was sharing his or her child's accomplishments with you, you might see that parent as bragging. Another person, who is not depressed, might simply view the parent as taking a valid interest and pleasure in his or her child's achievements.

Q My father no longer encourages me to do better. Could he be depressed?

It could be a possibility. If your father has other signs and symptoms of depression, he may have a depressive attitude summed up by the sentiment: "What's the use; nothing succeeds, so why even try?" He may also have lost the ability to experience the pleasure that a parent gets when his or her child succeeds.

Feelings

Q **My partner is depressed. Why does he always seem to get angry or ignore me?**

If your partner's depression is characterized by anhedonia, he will not be able to take pleasure from anything. Moreover, if you are trying to please him or coax him out of his depression, he may feel guilty and worthless for not being able to respond to you. He may also feel critical of you for making him feel bad. It's a sad paradox, but if you are asking your partner to feel good, you are actually making him feel bad. This could explain why he gets angry or ignores you.

Q **Since my wife got depressed, she has stopped hoping for another child. Why would she just give up?**

Hope is often one of the last feelings that depressed people lose. Without it, one is not likely to make much progress. Hopefulness drives us, while hopelessness renders us stagnant. Hopelessness is even a risk factor for suicide. Helplessness, which is often associated with hopelessness, may also be playing a role here.

Q **Why do I feel guilty about everything when I am depressed?**

The emotion of guilt tends to become stronger in some people when they are depressed, although it is not related to anything they have done. You could speculate, for example, that your depression might be triggered by the loss of a parent, and that you never worked through the emotion of guilt at the time of the loss. However, there is usually no satisfactory answer to be found. It is as if the network of brain cells that express guilt is firing at a high rate, even though there is nothing you did to cause this. Some people who are depressed have a feeling of guilt about "everything".

Q Is grouchiness a sign of depression?

It can be – grouchiness is an emotional state in which a person gets irked with very little provocation. It is a manifestation of frustration and anger. Sigmund Freud, the famous 19th-century psychoanalyst, thought of depression as anger turned inward, which might be the case much of the time. However, depressed people have also been known to turn anger outward, whether by being irritable or grouchy, or in other ways. Although grouchiness is commonly associated with older people, there are young grouches too, as parents of disaffected teenagers will testify.

THE IMPACT OF DEPRESSION ON FEELINGS

Most people with depression express their emotions in a different way from usual. Even though, most of the time, the main feeling tends to be one of depression, other emotions such as anxiety, anger, guilt, and sadness may also surface.

FEELING	IMPACT OF DEPRESSION
Anxiety	You may feel more anxious or handle anxiety less well than usual.
Anger	You may bottle up anger and find that it comes out in blasts or at unexpected times.
Sadness	You may feel sad or you may cry at the least provocation, without being able to pinpoint the reason.
Guilt	You may feel more guilty than usual, although you may not know why.
Joy	Feelings of joy may be completely absent, although depressed people do hold onto feelings of pleasure about their children.

Myth "People who are depressed don't get angry"

Truth People with depression often appear passive and withdrawn, which according to Freud's hypothesis are manifestations of anger turned inwards. While this may or may not be the case, depressed people do get angry and they often express anger inappropriately. The sullen depressive might lash out at surprising times, and about matters that others would consider inconsequential. Anger is present in people who have depression, but it is handled differently – and often ruinously.

Q Why is it that since my mother died, I feel like I don't know what to do?

Depression doesn't always result from losing someone close to you, but it may be the case in your situation, especially if you have some of the other signs and symptoms of depression. Try changing the words: "what to do?" to "where to turn?" and this will help you to find an answer. You have had a major loss, because of which you are feeling lost. This is very common in depression.

Q Why do I cry about things that never used to bother me?

Crying and feelings of sadness can be characteristic of depression. You may also find that tears may accompany various emotions, such as anger, and not just sadness alone. Some people describe their emotions as being all over the place when they are depressed.

Q My husband says he feels depressed, but he looks his usual self and even smiles when he tells me this. Is he really depressed?

He certainly could be depressed. There are 2 major ways of describing emotion: mood and affect. Mood is what a person experiences inside; what is actually felt by the person. Affect is what an observer sees. Thus, one can feel depressed and not look depressed – and vice versa. One can even have a concomitant emotion such as embarrassment when feeling certain emotions, and give an embarrassed smile. Your husband may be exhibiting what is known as inappropriate affect – or in lay terms, "smiling depression". When a person's descriptions of their feelings differ from their appearance, it is called mood incongruence. Inappropriate affect is one kind of mood incongruence. One of its causes is embarrassment. Part of the work of psychotherapy is to make mood and affect congruent and to resolve inappropriate affect. Then there is a better chance of progress in depression and other conditions.

Love, sex, and self-esteem

Q Since I've been depressed I feel as though I've fallen out of love with my partner. Is this normal?

Romantic love is a relatively new concept, and mostly a Western one. Couples fall in love, which is sometimes considered another term for infatuation, and then they either settle into a less intense state of intimacy and commitment or they choose to break up. When intimacy and commitment have been established, you can still derive a sense of closeness and pleasure from each other's company, without the infatuated, idealized perception of each other. When this sense of pleasure is lost, people often describe the sensation as falling out of love. Yet this loss of pleasure can also be a result of depression, since it can diminish your ability to get pleasure from things that you previously found pleasurable. What you have lost is the capacity to love – something that is regainable with time or treatment. This is why, when one partner is depressed, important decisions such as separation and divorce might best be deferred.

Q How does depression lead to the break-up of relationships?

Depression often brings about changes in a person's personality or behaviour. He or she may withdraw socially, desire solitude, and even lose the ability to feel love. The depressed person may also become more critical and argumentative. These changes can leave his or her partner feeling isolated, unloved, or even under attack. Add in the effects of disinterest from the depressed person – both in the relationship and in having sex – and the tolerance of the partner can be greatly stretched. Either partner may be the one to initiate a break-up.

Q Is it common for people to lose interest in sex when they are depressed?

It is all too common. Whether from the inability to experience pleasure (anhedonia), inability to feel love, social withdrawal, or something more direct, interest in sex (libido) is frequently diminished in depression. It is not something individuals can help, even with effort. They might go through the motions, but true interest is not there.

Q Should I tell my husband I'm so depressed I don't want to have sex?

You and your husband are actually fortunate in that you want to tell him about your problem. If you don't, he could sense your disinterest – as he probably already has – and interpret it in any number of ways. If you tell your husband it is part of your depression, you at least clarify the reasons for him and prevent him from feeling unloved or even suspecting that you are having an affair. If he can accept your depression for the clinical problem it is, he might even accommodate you and try to help you with your depression. Honesty is generally the best policy, especially as he is probably already aware of your disinterest.

Q When I was depressed, I had no interest in sex. Now I'm better, I want to have sex but it's not happening. Why?

Initially, you may have lost your libido due to depression. Then, if you took antidepressants, it is likely that they interfered with your sexual performance. Some men get erections, but have trouble ejaculating or having an orgasm while they are on antidepressant medication. Others have trouble maintaining an erection at all. If this is the case, tell your doctor; he or she can probably prescribe a different antidepressant. The situation is similar for women, who experience decreased ability to lubricate or achieve orgasm. Though more easily masked, the woman can be just as frustrated.

Q I'm divorced and my youngest child has just become a teenager. Why can't I bring myself to socialize or even date?

You have entered a stage of your life that requires fundamental change. If you are lonely or have experienced some loss, you would expect your confidence in dating or socializing to be low. However, if your self-esteem is too low, you may have a mild depression. Low self-esteem from depression can stop you from pursuing, let alone achieving, your goal of curing your loneliness. This is a vicious cycle – your low self-esteem prevents you from curing your loneliness, and your loneliness worsens your depression and erodes your self-esteem further.

Q I used to be a reasonably confident teacher. Since my depression, I can hardly face my students. Why?

Your self-esteem or self-confidence might have diminished, which is one of the hallmarks of depression. It is often accompanied by a vague sense of guilt, generally without having done anything wrong. Many people with depression feel guilty and consider themselves and what they do worthless.

Q Why does my partner insist on making me feel bad just because he feels depressed?

Your partner is probably using a psychological defence mechanism known as projection. He imagines his negative thoughts and feelings are what you are thinking or feeling; it is as if he is throwing them onto you in an attempt to get rid of them. So, when he feels depressed, incompetent, and worthless, he throws this on to you and considers you incompetent and worthless. This kind of defence does not work very well, because it drives other people away. It thus creates even more stress for the person who is projecting. Many people project chronically, not just when they are depressed. The insightful recipient quickly sees it as a reflection of the criticizer rather than of themselves.

Appetite and energy

Q How does depression affect appetite?

Depression can cause a marked gain or a marked loss in appetite. This may be accompanied by weight gain or weight loss. Some people with decreased appetite force themselves to eat, though the thought of food nauseates them. On the other hand, those with increased appetite might lack the will to eat more healthily.

Q Why did I lose my appetite yet put on weight during my depression?

This occurs quite frequently. Many people with depression will complain of lowered appetite, yet they gain weight. A possible reason could be that they may choose fattening foods, and are also less likely to exercise. However, little is known about this phenomenon.

Q Does a doctor take appetite changes into account when making a diagnosis for depression?

Yes. Changes in appetite, together with changes in sleeping patterns, are known as vegetative signs. This term can be somewhat confusing because signs are usually those aspects of a condition that can be independently observed. Therefore, sleep and appetite changes are more accurately called symptoms because they depend on a person reporting them – a doctor can observe neither. In any case, a doctor will certainly take appetite changes into account, although, as yet, there is little understanding of why they occur during depression.

Q Is it normal for depression to take away my energy?

Yes. Having low energy or no energy – called anergia – is common in depression. You may find it difficult to get up and get going. Coupled with lowered motivation, this can make you increasingly inactive.

Q **Why do I feel worse at certain times of the day?**

Depressed people usually experience some variation in energy levels throughout the day, and this is known as diurnal variation. Sometimes, at the worst point of a depression, a person will complain of his or her symptoms throughout the day.

Q **Do depressed people tend to struggle in the mornings?**

Generally, it is the morning, but it can also be the middle or the second half of the day. I had a patient who drank 15 cups of coffee at work in the morning and then, at about noon, finally got his energy levels up. He attributed this recovery to the coffee, when actually it was the fact that the morning was over. Since people cannot stop drinking coffee suddenly, I suggested my patient spread out his coffee intake over the course of the day. As it turned out, he didn't need coffee after the morning – the morning was simply the time when his depression affected him most.

Q **My depressed partner seems to be getting more active in the evenings, yet she won't admit to this improvement. Why?**

When depression starts to lift, the symptoms lessen during the person's "good" part of the day. However, rather than highlighting this improvement, depressed people tend to emphasize the times of the day when they still feel bad. For this reason, I have stopped asking patients whether they feel better during a certain part of the day. They'll say there is no such part of the day. Instead, I ask them when they feel worse. If they feel worse at a particular time, they will tell me. In either case, I've diagnosed their diurnal variation. It is as if they feel less uncomfortable focusing on the negative – the time of day they feel worse. It is unclear if this is due to anhedonia (inability to experience pleasure) or not.

Sleep and rest

Q **Why are changes in sleep patterns an important symptom of depression?**

Sleep changes are very important in diagnosing depression because almost every other symptom and sign could involve another factor. For example, low energy levels could be due to physical illness, decreased ability to concentrate could be due to family distractions, and low self-esteem could reflect real problems at work. However, sleep changes occur in the middle of the night, when the influence of other factors is minimal. Once other reasons for waking up in the middle of the night, such as pain or the urge to urinate, are ruled out, depression can often be ruled in.

Q **I can fall asleep, but why can't I stay asleep?**

This is called middle awakening (or middle insomnia) and describes waking up in the middle of the night. Assuming it is spontaneous and not the result of pain, the need to urinate, or a nightmare, middle awakening is quite characteristic of depression.

Q **Why am I so tired, even after the rare nights when I sleep through?**

Tiredness and not sleeping through the night are 2 key symptoms of depression and as you have noticed, they are not always related. Even when your sleep is occasionally fine and you are not expecting to be tired the next day, you are. This lowered energy can be common in depression, regardless of how well you sleep. When celebrities are admitted to hospital for depression-related conditions, this is sometimes referred to as "exhaustion". Exhaustion is a far less stigmatized term than depression, yet it is an honest description of a true depressive symptom: low energy.

What are terminal and initial insomnia?

A common occurrence in depression, terminal insomnia describes waking up too early and not being able to go back to sleep. It is also called early morning rising, or EMR. On the other hand, initial insomnia, which is difficulty in falling asleep, is more characteristic of anxiety than depression.

Q Why do I sleep during the day, but not at night?

You have a reversed sleep pattern, which commonly occurs in depression. Sometimes, people will wake up very early and watch the clock, hoping to fall asleep – as soon as the alarm rings, they become sleepy. Although people usually sleep less during depression, the opposite may also happen. The important thing is to look for a change in your sleeping pattern.

Q Why do I feel like I haven't slept at all, even though my wife says I have?

It sounds as though you do not have restful sleep. Lack of sound sleep can be very disturbing to people, both because they don't feel refreshed, and because others don't believe that their claims to tiredness are justified.

Q If I wake up at night, can I take a sleeping pill?

Generally, the effect of sleeping pills lasts for about 4 hours. If you wake up early and have more than 4 hours before you need to get up again, taking a sleeping pill should not be a problem. However, if you take a sleeping pill too close to your wake-up time, you will feel drugged or hungover in the morning.

Q Why couldn't I sleep well even after my depression lifted?

This is not an unusual pattern. It is likely that your depression did not fully lift. Sleep is a very sensitive monitor for progress in depression. This is because out of all the symptoms of depression, sleep is least affected by the external, daytime environment.

Q **My husband snores all night in stops and starts, and is so sleepy during the day that he drives badly. Is this a sign of depression?**

It sounds as though your husband has sleep apnoea, which is different from depression. When people have this condition, their airways become partially blocked, which is why you hear snoring. When your husband stops snoring, he is probably not breathing at all. After some seconds, he starts breathing – and snoring – again. In the morning, people with sleep apnoea feel tired, one reason why the condition can be confused with depression. Some people get sleep apnoea if they put on a lot of weight. Sometimes, the only way to diagnose sleep apnoea is to arrange an overnight sleep study. The treatment for sleep apnoea consists of using a breathing machine at night, losing weight, and opening the airways by using other measures.

THE EFFECTS OF DEPRESSION ON SLEEP

Depression affects sleep in characteristic ways. Some of these sleep problems can also be caused by other conditions.

Initial insomnia Difficulty falling asleep. Usually anxiety, can be depression.

Middle insomnia Spontaneous awakening after being asleep (but not from a dream, pain etc). Usually a symptom of depression.

Terminal insomnia Awakening for good over 2 hours before wake-up time. Also called early morning rising (EMR). Usually a symptom of depression.

Reversed sleep pattern Very poor sleep at night with sleeping (napping) during the day. Usually a symptom of depression; other possible causes include shift work.

Nightmare Waking from a frightening dream with bodily effects (sweating, shaking, or palpitations). Usually from anxiety; can be from medical problems.

Middle awakening with dream carryover Waking from a dream but not realizing it was just a dream for over 10 seconds. Usually a symptom of depression with psychosis.

Health and mortality

Q Why do I find it so difficult to exercise and eat in a healthy way ever since I've been depressed?

Exercise can be helpful when you are depressed. It often provides an improved sense of well-being for a while, especially if it is prolonged or intense. However, when you are depressed, you tend to lose interest and motivation and, sometimes find it difficult to get out of the house, or even out of bed. The motivation to exercise can be especially hard to find. The same applies to diet – depressed people often stop adhering to a healthy diet. This can lead to weight gain, which can impact negatively on your overall health.

Q Why does my wife complain of every little ache and pain since she has become depressed?

Your wife might be worrying more, or she could be somatizing. This means that she thinks she is medically ill, when the problem is actually psychological. To some extent this is a defence mechanism – it's always easier to think you have something you don't. More often, however, she does feel those aches and pains more. People in such situations may consult their doctor about the physical symptoms. After examinations and tests have ruled out a medical illness, a doctor will consider psychological causes. Somatization is one of these.

Q Can physical illness be caused or worsened by depression?

Yes, depression can cause or worsen headaches and affect blood pressure. Colds and other illnesses that are linked to the immune system are thought by many to be more frequent in depressed people. Fibromyalgia – a condition that involves chronic pain and fatigue – may be due to depression, but this remains controversial. Almost all illnesses will feel worse in a patient who is depressed.

Q **My husband drinks because he is depressed. Could this make him ill?**

Illness as a result of drinking is an indirect effect of depression, but one that is very real. Alcohol can lead to or worsen a host of medical conditions. Ulcers that were dormant can begin to bleed again; seizure disorders that were under control can flare up again; and individuals become more prone to falls and accidents, leading to musculoskeletal problems.

Q **Is it common to start smoking again during depression?**

Yes, people who have smoked in the past often resume smoking when they become depressed. People who are depressed tend to be anxious and, to some extent, nicotine lowers this anxiety, providing the smoker with momentary relief. Smoking also gives people something to do with their hands. You may smoke because you have lost interest in taking care of your health, which frequently happens in some forms of depression. Interestingly, some people *stop* smoking when they are depressed, although this usually happens at the point when they are coming out of their depression. There is an antidepressant, bupropion (Wellburtin), that can lower the urge to smoke.

Q **My teenage daughter has stopped looking after herself since she broke up with her boyfriend. Should I worry?**

You are right in focusing on this change in your daughter's behaviour. If she is depressed, it can lead to a loss of interest in many things that she enjoyed earlier, including her own well-being. This can manifest itself in several ways. Your daughter may abuse alcohol and/or drugs, and she may even drive after drinking. She may not care enough to think about her personal safety when she goes out. All of these things can have an impact on your daughter's health and even mortality.

Q How does severe depression affect a person's health?

Inattentiveness towards health concerns is a major characteristic of severe depression. If a depressed person has a pre-existing medical condition, he or she may neglect to look after it. The person might miss doses of medication, have trouble adhering to special diets, and be otherwise less able to cooperate with a doctor's advice. Depressed people may also take up potentially harmful habits, such as drinking, smoking, or overeating, which can further damage their health. Several studies show a higher rate of mortality from medical conditions in people who have depression. From heart disease to kidney disease, the risk of dying is greater if depression is present.

Q Depression has led my wife to stop taking her blood pressure pills. What should I do?

This is not at all uncommon. Depressed people often lose interest and motivation when it comes to taking medications for medical conditions. I had to hospitalize a depressed patient once because she could not/would not take antibiotics for an infection, which then spread to her blood. You should encourage your wife to take her pills. If she resists and gets angry, you need to proceed carefully. You could call her doctor and let him or her know. Doctors can listen to what callers say without needing the permission of their patients.

Q My mother lives alone and is depressed. Why can't she take her pills properly?

Depression lowers the ability to concentrate, so this could be one reason; another could be that she no longer cares about looking after herself. She could also have some passive suicidal thoughts – that is, although she might not actively commit suicide, she would not mind if she died as an indirect result of taking her medication incorrectly.

Q Physiotherapy helped my lower back pain – until I got depressed. Why the change?

People with depression tend not to expend as much effort on things, even if it results in pain. You could be working less hard in your physiotherapy sessions or you could be missing appointments. Ask your physiotherapist for feedback on this.

Q My cancer was under control, but it returned during my depression. Is there a connection?

There is a theory that distress lowers the body's immune function, which makes it easier for tiny cancers to enlarge. Although this is a controversial subject, many a doctor has noted the emergence of cancers when a person is depressed. However, there is currently no scientific consensus about the connection between depression and cancer.

Q My mother became depressed after her stroke. How does this affect her chances of recovery?

The link between depression and stroke is well established – it is estimated that one-third of the people who have stroke will develop depression. Their mortality rate is increased when compared to stroke victims without depression. Today, most doctors look for and treat depression in people who have had a stroke.

Q My diabetes is out of control ever since my depression started. Why?

There is no known direct link between depression and worsening diabetes. Instead, an indirect cause is likely. It may be that your depression has led you to pay less attention to your day-to-day diabetes routine, to your diabetic diet and medications. For example, if you are finding it difficult to concentrate, you could be using the wrong dose of insulin. Also, sometimes people who have depression find it hard to stay motivated or just don't care about themselves. They often let little things slip in their medical regimens and as a result, their medical condition worsens.

Daily activities

Q How does day-to-day life change during depression?

Depressed people slowly – or sometimes quickly – start to function less well. Their concentration levels may drop, which means they become slower and less effective at tasks both at home and at work. They may care less about themselves and their environment, so they may look unkempt or may stop tidying up at home. They may prefer isolation to interaction, so may stay at home alone. Parents may become less attentive to their children – they may stop helping with homework, for example. These are just a few of the changes that can happen during depression.

Q My husband has stopped shaving and caring about personal hygiene. Is that a sign of depression?

It could be. People who are depressed may shower or bathe less often than they did previously. Dental hygiene can be neglected as well. Men may stop shaving and grow a beard. If other aspects of your husband's life are deteriorating, this strengthens the possibility that he is depressed.

Q Why is my partner neglecting her appearance?

Lack of care and motivation regarding one's appearance is characteristic of depression. It takes lots of effort just to appear presentable in modern society, especially for women. Previously well-coiffed women will tie back or stop washing their hair. If your partner did her nails, she may stop. It's also common for depressed people to gain weight and pay less attention to their clothes – stylish people may become frumpy, and clothes may be chosen without thought or care. These changes usually happen gradually.

Q My son has stopped washing or shaving, but he won't admit that anything is wrong. Why?

Some depressed people rationalize the change in their personal habits by arguing, for example, that it is more economical to shower less frequently or that keeping a beard is simply a style preference. If this is the case with your son, it can be more difficult to understand his behaviour. If you say he is depressed, while he says he's not, you're at a stalemate – or an argument.

Q I'm starting to let things slide now that I'm depressed. Is this common?

Yes. Your depression is getting the better of you. It has diminished your will to help yourself, improve your life, and feel good. It leaves you doing worse and feeling worse. You may be dropping small but positive habits such as laying out your clothes before you go to bed at night, mowing the lawn, doing household repairs, and taking exercise. You may even be less bothered about things such as wearing a seatbelt when you drive.

Q Is it normal for work to become a struggle during depression?

Most people who are depressed continue to work, for both the economic and the social benefits that it provides. However, the pace and productivity of their work diminish. Concentration problems make it more difficult to do things such as filing, planning, problem-solving, and report writing. Deadlines become more difficult to meet. Not caring about work or about work relationships makes it more of a challenge to accomplish things. Depressed people are more likely to make mistakes at work, with consequences of varying severity. Until treatment for depression starts to take effect, it is advisable to eliminate any unnecessary work, to take on only simple tasks, and to tell your employers you are under personal stress. Many employers will lighten your workload, at least for a while.

Q I used to love shopping. Why has this changed?

If you are depressed, you may have lost interest or pleasure in a number of things that you used to enjoy doing before. On the other hand, if you become nervous when shopping and you go in and out of shops quickly, you might be showing signs of agoraphobia. This is an anxiety condition triggered by going out, shopping, waiting, queues, and crowds. It occurs frequently in conjunction with depression. Shopping is a daily activity, and depression – and its partner, anxiety – often interfere with it.

Q I've lost control of my finances. Is this common in depression?

People who are usually self-disciplined when it comes to their finances may lose this positive habit when they become depressed. Things may deteriorate to such an extent that even when their cheques start bouncing, they may fail to take control of the situation.

Q My teenage son just sits around and won't do his homework – what is wrong with him?

There could be several reasons why your son is sitting around and not doing his homework. Labels such as "couch potato" or "lazy" are used so frequently for adolescents that they seem normal. However, if your son was previously active and attentive to his work, his current inactivity could be a result of depression. Depression diminishes energy and lowers motivation, which often tend to result in behaviour that appears lazy. Your son's ability to concentrate may also be affected. This would make doing his homework difficult, even if he felt motivated. Most episodic depressions resolve with time, but school terms pass quickly. For this reason, you might want to seek prompt treatment before your son's school performance starts to deteriorate.

Q Why do I burn food and cook badly when I'm depressed?

Cooking is an activity that requires co-ordination and attention to timing. During depression your concentration may be less than what it would normally be. If you are distracted, for example, by a phone call, you might not remember to check the oven again. Positive habits, such as double checking things or keeping to a checklist, could also deteriorate. You might also be burning the food due to disinterest. Depressed people tolerate imperfection in many ways. After all, if you don't care about much, it doesn't matter if a meal is cooked well.

Q My husband watches TV late into the night, then complains he is sleepy the next day. Why doesn't he listen to my advice?

This pattern is not uncommon in people who have depression. Many people do not even try to fall asleep at their usual bedtime. Instead, they find ways to stay awake. Of course, their complaints of sleepiness the next day fall on deaf ears – until their family members realize that this behaviour is often a part of depression. They can then encourage treatment.

LOSS OF INTEREST IN DAILY ACTIVITIES

Diminished interest in things that were previously of interest is a key criterion for a diagnosis of depression. Activities that often suffer during depression include:

- Showering/shaving
- Attention to oral hygiene
- Hair/nail care
- Attention to clothing

- Preparing food
- House cleaning
- Taking the rubbish out
- Taking exercise
- Taking medication

- Doing the laundry
- Socializing
- Completing work or schoolwork
- Care of children

Alcohol and drug abuse

Q Could I be drinking more due to depression?

This may well be the case. People who are depressed may drink to calm the dull or acute pain of depression, to allow their depressive feelings to express themselves, or to increase their sense of well-being. Not caring about your life or your health is another factor that may drive you to drink more.

Q If alcohol helps in depression, why not use it?

Drinking alcohol to make yourself feel better is described as self-medication – this means the use of non-prescribed substances to treat an otherwise treatable condition. You probably self-medicate in other ways as well. For example, if you have a cold, you might go to a pharmacy and buy a medicine for it without consulting your doctor. In the latter case, you know you have a medical condition, but realize it is temporary and mild – it is simpler and faster to self-medicate than to see a doctor. With alcohol, however, the cost of self-medication is high in terms of health, family relationships, and work life. Moreover, the side effects of alcohol can be severe, from car accidents, to falling, to behaving in ways that you may regret later.

Q Why do people self-medicate when this causes more damage?

People may drink because they feel low. If they notice that drinking diminishes such feelings or elevates their mood, they keep doing it. This is because, often, the depressed feeling is not perceived as a medical condition. If people thought they had a condition that was treatable, they would usually go to a doctor. However, a depressed feeling is often considered just that; and if alcohol alleviates it, the rationalization goes, "Why not have a drink?"

Q Why did my mother's doctor recommend a glass of sherry before bedtime?

Your mother's doctor might not have been able to prescribe the many sleeping pills that are available now. More than likely, however, he or she understood that your mother might have been more comfortable with a natural substance in the form of alcohol rather than a pill. In either case, your mother was not self-medicating – she was following her doctor's prescription. She may have done the same thing on her own, of course.

Q Don't some people treat themselves for depression with prescription medication?

All too many people do just that. These are not drug abusers – just average people, who happen to have a medical condition that requires sedating or pain-killing medication. Alongside this condition, they also have undiagnosed depression. Over time, people notice that their depressed feelings (from the undiagnosed depression) abate when they take their medication. This may lead to people taking their medication more often than they need to or becoming addicted to it. Sometimes doctors are able to spot depression when people ask for more and more refills of their sedating or pain-killing medication.

Q Why do some people self-medicate with street drugs?

Generally, people do this when they have not been prescribed medications that might give them the same effect. While some people would never use street drugs on principle, others do not care.

Q What types of drugs might depressed people abuse?

Depressed people might prefer an "upper", like cocaine. Agitated people might prefer a "downer", like a barbiturate, or an anxiolytic, like diazepam (Valium) or alprazolam (Xanax). Still others take one drug to get up and another to come down. Faster-acting drugs tend to be preferred to slower, longer-lasting ones.

Suicide

Q Are people who commit suicide always mentally ill?

Not all people who kill themselves have mental health problems, for example, Japanese suicidal pilots – kamikazes – in World War II and suicide bombers. Some people with terminal illnesses and, presumably, no history of mental health problems, have also been suicidal – this includes those assisted in suicide by some doctors. Until the recent advances in treatment, some people with AIDS have also been suicidal.

Q What is the most common reason for commiting suicide?

Depression certainly accounts for the majority of suicides, although many of these cases never received treatment. Both psychosis and panic disorder increase the risk of suicide. The final trigger that pushes someone to commit suicide is generally difficult to determine. However, the reasons given by people whose suicide attempts fail include: avoidance of intolerable psychological pain, such as loss of a relationship or chronic depressive feelings; attempts to influence others, such as forcing a girlfriend to return; feelings of helplessness and hopelessness; a recent significant loss; and alcohol or substance abuse.

Q Don't some people make false attempts at suicide?

Yes. They may be trying to manipulate someone close to them. For example, they might take an excess of pills when they know a loved one will return home soon, find them, revive them, and show them the love and attention they desire. Unfortunately, if the loved one is delayed, the plan can backfire, and they will not be rescued from death.

Q Can the tendency to commit suicide run in my family?

If your family had lots of cases of depression, there could be a higher rate of suicide in your family. However, suicide rates are actually so low in terms of the general population that it is difficult to find more than 2 or 3 cases of suicide in any family over the generations.

Q Why are alcohol, drug use, and psychosis risk factors?

Alcohol and drugs lower the ability of the mind to function properly. Psychosis also has the same effect. People say and do things in intoxicated or psychotic states that they would not otherwise. For example, the logic that one will have diminished pain at the expense of being dead forever, is lost on someone who is psychotic or influenced by a substance. Alcohol and drugs also lower the anxiety associated with suicide and death. Anxiety usually protects people from acting on their impulses – without it, they act.

Q What is the frequency of suicide?

Although statistics from different studies vary, the frequency of suicide in the general population is about 0.01 per cent, or 10 per 100,000 people per year. However, in the case of certain subsets of the population, the frequency is greater. These subsets include people who are depressed (the rates are between 10–30 times higher) and elderly men (the rates are about 5 times higher). Even though the suicide rates might seem dramatically higher among depressed people, it still means that more than 99 per cent of people with depression do not commit suicide in a given year. Overall, suicide is the 11th leading cause of death in the UK. However, among people between 15–24 years of age, it is the third leading cause of death.

Myth "You'd have to be crazy to think of suicide"

Truth Suicide has been regarded as a sin by most religions and a derangement by most cultures. Others, in certain situations, have blessed it. In any case, just thinking about suicide, called suicidal ideation, is so common under stress that it is difficult to call it crazy or abnormal. Acting on these thoughts, however, is when a person's state of mind must be in question.

Q Why do people try but fail to commit suicide more than once?

As people move from not feeling suicidal to feeling suicidal, a state of ambivalence occurs. On the one hand, they want to die, but on the other they don't. It is this ambivalence that leads to a lot of failed suicides. When the ambivalence is between the wish to die and the fear of dying, some people drink alcohol to suppress their fear. Although it is easy physically to commit suicide, it is psychologically difficult to resolve the state of ambivalence.

Q Do men commit suicide more often than women?

In the developed world, women attempt suicide more often than men – about 3 times as often in the UK – but men successfully commit suicide about 4 times more often than women. However, the reasons why women fail to commit suicide are still unclear.

Q Can doctors predict who is likely to commit suicide?

Doctors use statistical data to identify the risk factors for suicide. They also use common sense. So if a person expresses suicidal thoughts, called suicidal ideation, a doctor would explore this. See the chart on the risk factors for suicide on p103.

Q How can a doctor tell when a suicidal person is no longer at risk?

It can be very difficult to determine when a person is no longer contemplating suicide. Someone who really wants to commit suicide may readily lie to a doctor about his or her real thoughts. A family member may be a good judge of whether the person has genuinely moved beyond the risk of suicide. A doctor will look for a diminishment in various risk factors in order to discharge a person from hospital. This might mean a psychosis being treated or the beginning of an alcohol cessation program. Also, if the stress that triggered the suicide attempt is reduced, the risk becomes less.

Q Our son accused us of thinking he was going to overdose. Was he suicidal?

"Suicidal" is a term with several meanings, ranging from thinking about suicide to being on the verge of committing suicide. Your son could have been testing your reactions, trying to scare you, or projecting his own thoughts about suicide onto you. Projecting in this instance means that he was considering an overdose himself but projected the thought onto you. Any talk of suicide implies that the person is in distress, and this should be taken seriously.

Q My daughter repeatedly puts herself in dangerous situations. Could she be suicidal?

Sometimes, people who are depressed are inattentive to danger in their surroundings. As a result they may get injured at work or have accidents. However, if your daughter is deliberately creating or putting herself in dangerous situations, she may be suicidal. This is not much different from a situation called in the US "suicide by cop", in which a person commits an infraction or crime, and then, literally, asks the police to go ahead and shoot him. This should be taken very seriously.

Q My father is 85 and ill. He told me he wouldn't mind dying. Is he suicidal?

He has, at the very least, passive suicidal ideation. This means that he wouldn't mind dying, but he wouldn't do anything to speed it up. This is very common, especially in frail, elderly people. In most such cases, family members find themselves unable to discuss thoughts of suicide with the elderly person, leaving him or her very alone.

Q Why do some people cut themselves?

Some people cut or otherwise mutilate themselves, without necessarily wanting to die. Discussions with these people reveal several reasons, such as wanting to see blood or feel pain to be sure they are alive.

SUICIDE RISK FACTORS

The assessment of whether someone is suicidal is the most critical any mental health professional has to make. Many risk factors are obvious, such as suicidal statements. Others, such as a history of violence, have been recognized only by experts. The following list does not attempt to rank the risk factors – more than one factor is generally present simultaneously.

BIOLOGICAL FACTORS
- Age (adolescents, elderly)
- Sex (women try more; men succeed more)

VERBALIZATIONS
- Talk of suicide in general
- Passive suicidal ideation
- Active suicidal ideation
  - suicidal intent
  - suicidal plan or note
    - means to carry out the plan

PSYCHOSOCIAL TRIGGERS
- Isolation
  - Chronic
  - Acute
    - The final relationship
- Life events
- Loss of relationship/parent/child
- Family history of suicide
- Peer suicide (copy-cat, in adolescence)

PERSONALITY FACTORS
- Aggressiveness
- Impulsivity
- Violence

BUILDING UP BEHAVIOUR
- Re-arranging personal affairs, such as will or insurance
- Moving the means of suicide closer
- Prior suicidal behaviour/attempt

LOWERED BARRIER TO SUICIDAL ACTION
- Alcohol use
- Drug use
- Psychosis

LEGAL ISSUES
- Bankruptcy
- Arrest
- Incarceration
- Divorce

PARA-SUICIDAL BEHAVIOUR
- Inattentiveness
- Dangerous/risky behaviour
- Manipulativeness/suicidal gesture
- Ambivalent attempts
  - Superficial cutting
  - Small overdose

DIAGNOSES
- Mental illness
  - Depression
    - Hopelessness/helplessness
    - Setback after initial improvement
  - Panic disorder
  - Psychosis
    - Command auditory hallucinations to suicide
- Physical illness
  - Chronic
  - New diagnosis

Isolation

Q Why do people who are depressed become isolated?

They tend to become isolated voluntarily. This doesn't necessarily mean that they don't go out. It just means that they interact less, pull away from friends, and generally want to be alone. In contrast, many infirm people with illness-enforced isolation interact as often as possible. Unfortunately, illness-enforced isolation can also lead to depression, which can then lead to voluntary social isolation.

Q Don't socially isolated people get lonely?

Loneliness and isolation do not necessarily go hand in hand. Loneliness is the feeling of not being connected when one wants to be. People in bad marriages often feel lonely, even though they interact with their partners every day. At work, a person who is the only one with a particular skill can feel intellectually lonely in that he or she cannot discuss that skill with anyone. Depressed people who are alone voluntarily will not necessarily feel lonely.

Q Why does my mother want to be alone, even though she feels better after visiting friends or family?

This is one of the inconsistencies found in depression. Your mother will feel better, yet she won't willingly want to repeat the visits. The effort of interacting may be too much for her, even though she finds the result of the interaction pleasurable. It is important to encourage the highest level of function possible by encouraging her to go out. This works as a general rule. For example, there are claims that when depressed prisoners of war are encouraged to exercise, they feel better and do better.

Q My husband seems to be pulling out of social obligations one by one. Why?

Social isolation, like so many other signs and symptoms, generally develops gradually. At first, people continue to go out, whether to work, shop, or visit friends. Then, as they start to get less out of social interactions, they gradually withdraw. The chain of events may include your husband pulling away from people and social activities, then going out only for necessities, or not going out at all, then not getting dressed, then sitting around all day, and, eventually not even getting out of bed. Depression can cause this level of withdrawal – some people want to stop interacting so much, they precipitate a divorce. Then they are even more alone, which they might prefer, even though it is likely to worsen their depression.

Q Isn't social isolation bad for your health?

Yes, there are studies that confirm this. People who are socially isolated have a greater risk of developing heart attacks and stroke, for example. The inverse of this issue has also been explored: why does social interaction promote health? Although it seems intuitive that this would be the case, there are no good answers as to exactly why.

Q I had a panic attack when I was shopping and now I stay indoors all the time. I don't feel depressed, but could I be?

Not necessarily. As with so many other signs and symptoms, social isolation overlaps more than one condition. It sounds like you have a panic disorder with agoraphobia, which occurs quite frequently. If you like interacting with visitors, you are not socially isolated and you are not necessarily depressed. Staying indoors does not have to mean social isolation. For example, people who are housebound with a physical illness keep socially active by receiving visitors – they would not be considered socially isolated or depressed.

Vicious cycles

Q How do vicious cycles affect depressed people?

Anyone can get into a vicious cycle, but when people who have depression get into a vicious cycle it can intensify their depression. For example, a depressed person may drink alcohol to combat depression, only to discover that the negative effects of drinking make the depression worse. The worsening depression then causes the person to drink even more.

Q When my depressed, nursing-home bound mother shouts at me for being late, it discourages me from visiting her at all. What can I do?

Your mother is probably lonely and feels more so when you don't arrive on time. She becomes angry with you for making her frustrated, even though your visit could allow her to feel less lonely during and after it. Her anger is likely to alienate you and make the visit a frustrating experience for both of you. As a result, your motivation to visit promptly on the next occasion may be low. To get out of this vicious cycle you need to break down the steps of your interaction and find a way to stop the cycle (see the box on p107).

Q How can vicious cycles in depression be stopped?

Basically, vicious cycles in depression are not much different from other vicious cycles. They just have depressive themes. The task is to understand the cycle by defining what one person does that affects the other, then how the other responds to make the situation worse. You may be able to identify only 1 or 2 steps in the beginning, but the idea is to insert more and more steps into the cycle. This gives you more and more places to stop the cycle of events (see the box on p107).

HOW TO REVERSE A VICIOUS CYCLE IN DEPRESSION

These steps describe a vicious circle that might occur between a depressed woman and her husband. His motive is to please her, perhaps by buying presents or flowers, but this makes her uncomfortable and the interaction quickly becomes unpleasant.

AT THE MOMENT, THIS HAPPENS:

Step 1: he tries to please her.

Step 2: she criticizes his efforts.

Step 3: he tries harder.

Step 4: she reacts more strongly.

Step 5: he stops trying.

Result: both feel worse.

THIS IS WHAT HAPPENS IF YOU BREAK DOWN THE STEPS:

Step 1: he tries to please her.

Step 1A: she feels uncomfortable.

Step 1B: she feels angry with him for making her feel uncomfortable.

Step 1C: she wants him to stop making her uncomfortable.

Step 2: she criticizes his flower selection.

Now, because you know what is happening in detail between steps 1 and 2, it is possible to reverse the cycle.

You can test your steps by asking questions. For example: "Did my giving you a gift make you uncomfortable?" If you are right, you can keep going. For example: "What can I do to make you less uncomfortable?" The response to this might be: "Stop trying to please me so much." The man can then stop trying so hard in the wrong direction and as a result both husband and wife will feel less frustrated and the vicious cycle is stopped. Some of these steps may feel counterintuitive, so it is important to give them thought before acting.

Note: It is not a good idea to say to someone who is depressed, "What can I do to make you comfortable?" Depressed people often feel less comfortable if you try to make them more comfortable. This is why it is better to say: "What can I do to make you less uncomfortable?"

Work and career

Q How can depression affect my work?

A decreased ability to concentrate, brought on by depression, can slow down your pace at work or lead you to make more mistakes. Your workmates may get tired of picking up the slack, and bosses may get tired of decreased productivity. If you are irritable or withdrawn, your relationships with your workmates may be negatively affected. Finding the motivation to work is often difficult as well. In some cases, depressed people cannot get out of bed, which, of course, makes it impossible even to get to work.

Q Why can't I enjoy my work or the finished product anymore?

This is quite common in depression. The capacity to feel love, pleasure, and enjoyment is very frequently lost. People are often moved to be productive at work by the love of the work itself or its results. With these things gone, you are less motivated and productive, and as a result, you have even less to feel good about – if you only could. It is a vicious cycle.

Q My workmate is depressed – he drinks and calls in sick all the time. What can I do?

You can urge your workmate to seek treatment for his depression. Depressed people often drink, which leads to hangovers and calling in sick. When they return to work, they are greeted with anger by their employers. Eventually, the employer reacts to a final straw and fires the person. Even unions will not support employees with this pattern of behaviour. Some sophisticated employers with trained human resource departments may refer the person to a counsellor. However, all too often, the depressed person is fired for decreased performance.

Q How will mild depression affect my work?

In mild cases of depression, productivity is not always diminished and the degree to which you and your working relationships suffer is much less. In these cases, it is rare to lose your job as a result of depression.

Q I loved my work, until the company was restructured. Now I'm just stressed. Could I also be depressed?

Yes – take-overs and restructurings at work are often quite stressful and can lead to depression. This is generally due to personnel shifts, especially downsizing. With less people available to do the work, the "lucky" few survivors have more work to do. These kinds of changes often bring out smouldering, low-grade depressions, in which people are just about able to get by, even for years.

Q Is it possible that I'm depressed as a result of getting a new boss?

New bosses are often a source of stress at work. If the difficulty is a difference in work style or personality, you might feel stressed and even become depressed. However, if the new boss has a destructive style of management, the problem really lies with the boss and not with you. It is generally not until several employees react that something is changed. Unfortunately, you and several others will have suffered until then.

Q I've been laid off work. Now I can't even make myself look for a new job. Could I be depressed?

This pattern is common in depression. Depressed people often have a hard time being optimistic enough to believe that their efforts could lead to a job. At other times their amotivation or hopelessness keeps them from trying to make the effort. Low energy and social withdrawal can have the same result. In some cases, the depressed person answers a job ad and even goes for an interview but is let down by poor presentation or lack of concentration.

Treating depression yourself

There are plenty of self-help
techniques available for treating
depression. They range from relaxation
exercises to intense exercise. You can
also try to recognize and challenge
depressive or anxious thoughts,
and find more positive alternatives.
Self-help techniques can be used on
their own or in conjunction with the
treatment you receive from a doctor.

Self-help

Q Can I treat myself for depression?

Unless your depression is severe, there is usually no reason not to try whatever approach works for you. There are various reasons why people prefer self-help to consulting a doctor. Some people have difficulty accepting help from others because it makes them feel uncomfortable to be dependent. Others feel more in control if they can help themselves; helping oneself has been a maxim of society for centuries. Still other people try self-help techniques because they don't like going to doctors or because self-help techniques are easily available and inexpensive.

Q What kind of self-help techniques can help me with my depression?

One thing you can do is wait – most cases of depression resolve with time. The fact that you are looking for some kind of help, however, suggests that you feel you have waited long enough. You could try reading a self-help book on depression – those that emphasize a re-thinking of your depressive attitude may help. This re-thinking is part of cognitive-behavioural therapy (see pp136–139).

Q How will I know when to give up on self-help?

If you are not getting anywhere with any one approach, you should consider adding another or switching approaches. For example, if you started with self-help and found it useful up to a point, you could seek additional help from a doctor. This doesn't mean you have to discard your old approach entirely. For example, many people receive professional help in the form of psychotherapy, yet complement this with self-help. It is important, however, to let your doctor know what else you are doing.

Q Why don't doctors recommend self-help?

Doctors, in general, are data driven. If the data prove that a particular treatment works and its benefits outweigh the risks, they'll use that treatment. Getting reliable data, however, is more difficult than one would think. For example, each new medicine that comes on the market goes through a very costly and time-consuming series of experiments. For the many that start the process, only a few survive the scrutiny of scientific and regulatory approval. For all kinds of simple techniques, however, where the risks of side effects are low, the threshold is low for using them. Some techniques, such as relaxation, are gaining acceptance as more people use and benefit from them.

Q Are there any alternative treatments I could try?

Yes, there are various alternatives that you can try for your depression – these include intense exercise (see p125), herbal remedies, acupuncture, massage, yoga, and deep relaxation/stress management. These treatments must be used regularly to work, but so must antidepressant medication. If an alternative treatment works for you, there is no reason to stop it. In general, it is a good idea to let your doctor know about which alternative treatments you are using.

Q Do alternative treatments work?

Scientific studies have not shown alternative treatments to be effective in depression. However, you might get a placebo response (which means the treatment will work because you believe in its efficacy), which of course is better than no response. Alternative treatments are best used together with conventional medical treatment, as a partial response to each treatment might be better than a partial response to just one.

Social contact

Q When I am depressed, I want to be alone. Is there anything wrong with this?

Generally, you would be better off with some social contact. Keeping in regular contact with people has a number of social and psychological benefits. It also helps you to avoid the health problems associated with social isolation. Some surveys have shown that well-adjusted people have, on an average, 7 or so people in their social networks. These would be people to whom you could turn for a sounding board on a variety of problems. Just talking with someone you've developed a relationship with over time can help with problem solving in ways that books cannot. Often, talking to more than one person in one's social network is helpful, as any overlap in their responses would be more valid than otherwise.

Q Should I discuss my depression with friends or family?

To some extent, this should be determined by your relationship with people in your social network and family. There may be things you wouldn't trust anyone else to hear other than your family. Family members also are unlikely to reject you for your problems. On the other hand, family relationships are so important, many people will not want family members to know about their problems. For example, teenagers may fear their parents' response if they reveal certain things, such as drinking. Also, family members can have so much faith in you, that their responses aren't helpful. For example, if you are the successful one in the family and you become depressed, family members might tend to minimize the problem and reassure you that you'll get over it.

Q Since I've been depressed, I get along with my family better than with my friends. Why?

There could be many reasons for this. The relationships with family members are tied by blood and law. You can say and do more without the fear of losing your family. Also, family relationships originate long before friendships, at a time when you are vulnerable, dependent, and without the social skills needed to control negative interactions. Family members tend to tolerate more negative feelings than friends do. For example, you can tell your mother you are angry with her, and she won't/can't stop being your mother. A friend, however, can back away more easily. You can also express your frailties to your family, although you may receive pressure to reverse them.

Q I've spoken a lot to my best friend about my depression. Will I overburden her?

You certainly could. I have had patients who came for psychotherapy, having worn out their friends. Friends want to help, but there are limits to what they can offer. If the problem is severe or if it doesn't respond to your friend's suggestions, he or she may get frustrated. Speaking with other close friends might help. Ultimately, though, you don't want to push friends away in frustration. There is a point at which professional help is warranted.

Q Once I start psychotherapy, should I stop talking to my friends and family about my depression?

Not at all. As your therapy progresses, it is likely that you'll have different issues to talk about. Use good judgement, of course, as some things are so personal they best remain in the therapy. However, if you are exploring issues that relate to your parents and family, you might want to talk through these with your siblings. Often, significant progress is made by hearing another perspective on what went on in your family; how your parents might have treated you differently from other siblings; and how stress that you don't remember might have affected your upbringing.

Q Should I share my problems with people I meet on the Internet?

The Internet has revolutionized both the availability of information, as well as personal communication. One thing that makes Internet communication attractive is the anonymity it offers – you can keep your Internet conversations separate from the rest of your life. Another advantage is that the Internet is so widely used, you might find people with problems very similar to yours. There are chat rooms dedicated to many psychiatric diagnoses. For example, you can actually discuss your concentration problems with someone who has identical problems. However, it's also important to be aware that Internet friends might not be who they seem to be. Also, Internet friends are not the same as personal friends you meet face-to-face. There are advantages to both kinds of contact, and if you are careful, it is possible to gain from both.

Q How can voluntary work help?

Voluntary work is often quite rewarding personally. It lacks the competitiveness of the workplace, and one doesn't always have to attend when feeling bad. Whether the voluntary work is religious, charitable, or civic in orientation, it provides valuable social contact and the opportunity to make friends. However, if voluntary work provides only casual social contact, then this is generally not enough. You need a few close, trusting relationships for support. One cannot manage more than a few close friendships, since so much time is needed to cultivate them. Thus, it is important to choose a voluntary work in which there are people of the same age, interests, or religion. While the benefits of the work are important, they are outweighed by the opportunity for meaningful social contact.

Recognizing poor coping strategies

Q **What is maladaptive coping?**

When stress enters your life and changes your personal circumstances or environment, you need to adapt to that change using coping strategies. If you adjust well to your new circumstances, this is described as coping adaptively. If you don't adjust well, this is described as coping maladaptively.

Q **Why do coping strategies matter as long as I'm coping somehow?**

Maladaptive coping strategies can lead you into vicious cycles that, ultimately, may make your depression worse. For example, imagine that you are suffering from low motivation and energy, which makes it difficult for you to go to work. An adaptive coping method would be to take some time off or negotiate fewer assignments at work. A maladaptive coping method would be to quit your job. Although the latter solves the immediate problem, it leads to domestic, social, and financial stress, which, in turn, can deepen your depression.

Q **When my husband got depressed and started drinking again, was that maladaptive coping?**

If he was drinking to try to get rid of depressive feelings, he would be coping maladaptively. He was adjusting negatively to his new situation, that is, his life with depression. Alcohol would have worsened his condition. This kind of pattern tends to spiral out of control unless family and friends intervene successfully. You could try to make your husband aware of this, so that if he becomes depressed again, he can find better coping strategies.

Cascade of depression

In depression, seemingly innocuous events and situations can trigger negative thoughts and feelings that feed off each other until they spiral out of control. Interpreting the event or situation differently and in a positive light can prevent this cascade of depression. In the following examples, "thought" refers to your interpretation of an event and "feeling" refers to your reaction to the thought.

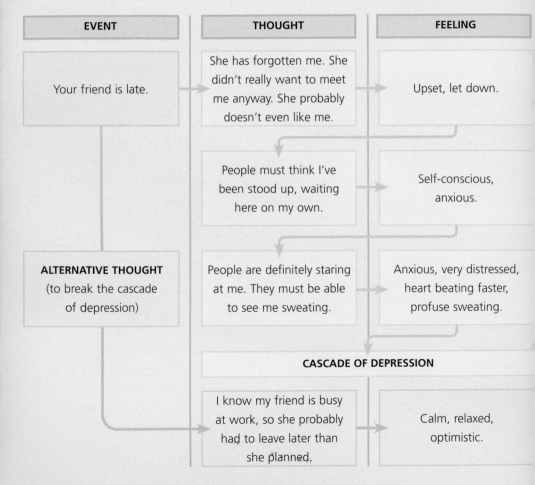

EVENT	THOUGHT	FEELING
Your friend is late.	She has forgotten me. She didn't really want to meet me anyway. She probably doesn't even like me.	Upset, let down.
	People must think I've been stood up, waiting here on my own.	Self-conscious, anxious.
ALTERNATIVE THOUGHT (to break the cascade of depression)	People are definitely staring at me. They must be able to see me sweating.	Anxious, very distressed, heart beating faster, profuse sweating.
	CASCADE OF DEPRESSION	
	I know my friend is busy at work, so she probably had to leave later than she planned,	Calm, relaxed, optimistic.

Q **I'm depressed after the death of my husband. I feel like packing up and starting a new life somewhere else. Will this help?**

This is called a "geographical cure" and it's another example of maladaptive coping. Geographical cures don't usually work and can actually worsen the problem. Moving to a new location involves losing social networks and service resources and contacts – everyone from your friends and family members to your doctor and car mechanic. You would need to re-establish all the connections that you have built up over years and this alone would add stress to your life. You are also likely to carry your depression with you, wherever you go.

Q **Is marrying on the rebound considered an example of maladaptive coping?**

In most cases, yes. The word "rebound" implies that the main reason for the new relationship is to cope with the loss of the old one. We all know that there is more to marriage than replacing a lost person. If the driving force behind the rebound marriage is to compensate for a loss, it is likely that you will want to go ahead regardless of its negative consequences. You will choose to overlook or minimize any factors that suggest the rebound marriage is a bad idea. Overlooking and minimizing factors that you should really take into account while making important decisions, are common examples of maladaptive coping.

Q **How can I learn better ways of coping with my problems?**

The first step is to learn to identify when you are coping maladaptively to the changes in your environment. If you are aware that your coping strategies are leading to vicious circles that actually worsen your depression, you can start to behave differently. Adaptive coping strategies involve seeking whatever help you need and using this help.

Positive coping strategies

Q **How can I stop thinking about everything in such a negative way?**

Negative thinking is a common feature of depression. It's easy to get into a cascade of negative thoughts that make you feel bad. Recognizing that such thoughts can trigger negative feelings is the first step to tackling this problem. Once you have identified the specific thoughts that are making you feel bad, you may be able to stop the cycle and search for alternative, more positive thoughts. See the chart on p118 for examples of this.

Q **What can I do to feel less anxious?**

You can identify the thoughts that cause you anxiety, challenge their validity, and search for alternative, more positive thoughts. You can also adopt a problem-solving approach by breaking down your anxiety into its basic components. First, is your anxiety based on a real threat? Second, what is the worst that could happen? Third, are there any practical ways of dealing with the perceived threat? Fourth, share the problem with someone you trust to get a different perspective. For more details on this approach see p121. Another, more general way of coping with anxiety is to relieve stress through practising yoga, meditation, or trying relaxation exercises (see p127).

Q **I can't sleep since I've been depressed. What can I do?**

There are several different sleep problems that can affect people who are depressed. For example, some people find it difficult to get to sleep, whereas others find it difficult to stay asleep. The former tends to be linked with anxiety and the latter with depression. The different types of sleep problem and the ways of dealing with them are described on pp122–123.

COPING WITH ANXIETY

If you are faced with a stressful problem, threatening situation, or worrying event, it is normal to feel anxious. However, you need to recognize that it is the accompanying thoughts that fuel the anxiety, and not the situation or event itself. The following steps will help you to prevent anxiety from becoming more acute.

Take ownership	Does the problem really belong to you? Ask yourself if you are getting needlessly anxious over an event or situation that does not pose any threat to your well-being.
Articulate the problem	Put the problem into words and write down what you think is the essence of the problem and what could potentially be the worst-case scenario.
Find solutions	List as many ways as you can for solving the problem. Ask yourself which is the most practical solution, then break it down into manageable steps.
Discuss the problem	Describe your anxieties to a friend you can trust. Try to get a sense of perspective.
Manage your stress	Take steps to reduce your stress levels – for example, take regular exercise and practise relaxation, meditation, or visualization.

Coping with sleep problems

Several patterns of sleep disruption are found in depression. The key is that there is a *change* in sleep pattern for it to be included as a diagnostic criterion in depression. As with any medical sign or symptom, it is important to consider the possibility that there may be an alternative reason for your sleep problem – the sleep patterns listed here assume that pain or the need to urinate are *not* involved.

Sleep Pattern	Initial insomnia
Description	Difficulty falling asleep
Comment	Usually from anxiety
Tips	• Practise sleep hygiene. For example, don't drink caffeine or do any stimulating activities near bedtime. • Empty your bladder. • Dim the lights as bedtime approaches. • Practise deep relaxation while in bed. • Take sleeping pills or anti-anxiety (anxiolytic) medication if prescribed.
Sleep Pattern	Middle insomnia
Description	Awakening after falling asleep
Comment	Characteristic of depression
Tips	• Try not to get out of bed. • Practice deep relaxation. • Avoid turning on the lights. • Empty your bladder if you need to. • Avoid eating. • Take another sleeping pill only if needed and if you have more than 4 hours left before wake-up time (to avoid a hangover).
Sleep Pattern	Terminal insomnia
Description	Early morning rising, for example more than 2 hours before your desired wake-up time.
Comment	Major characteristic of depression
Tips	• Try not to turn on the lights. • Empty your bladder if you need to. • Try deep relaxation. • If needed, increase the dose of sleeping pills before sleep.

Sleep Pattern	Reversed sleep pattern
Description	Poor sleep at night with daytime napping
Comment	Frequently found in depression, though not diagnostic.
Tips	• Use the tips opposite to sleep at night. • Avoid daytime napping – keep lights bright, stay out of bed, and set an alarm if possible.

Sleep Pattern	Non-restorative sleep
Description	Sensation of not having slept
Comment	Not diagnostic of depression
Tips	• Try strategies similar to initial insomnia. • Sleeping pills may be needed prior to sleep.

Sleep Pattern	Nightmares
Description	Awakening from a frightening dream with shaking, palpitations, sweating, and hyperventilation.
Comment	More characteristic of anxiety than depression, for example post-traumatic stress disorder.
Tips	• Difficult to control by oneself. • Generally requires medication, especially small doses of antipsychotic medication/major tranquillizers prior to sleep.

Sleep Pattern	Sleep apnoea
Description	Sleep, alternating with non-sleep without awakening. Snoring reflects partial airway obstruction.
Comment	Not part of depression. Daytime sleepiness can lead to road accidents.
Tips	• This is a sleep disorder that requires laboratory diagnosis. • Treatment often requires breathing machine.

Diet and exercise

Q Are there diets that can help my depression?

There are no specific diets that have been proven to help depression. However, if you are overweight and feel it would enhance your self-esteem to lose weight, it can be worth trying. If you are successful, people are likely to compliment you and you may feel better as a result. Losing weight is also likely to make you feel healthier, which can make you feel better too. The problem with diets, however, is that they require lots of effort, motivation, and optimism. Unfortunately, these are things that diminish in depression. For example, it is difficult to stick to a diet if you don't have any hope that it will work or help. Relying on diet can also backfire, as failure will make a depressed person feel worse than before. It is better to take small steps that can be successful, than leaps that can fail.

Q Can taking dietary or herbal supplements help depression?

There have been claims that taking some vitamin supplements can help relieve premenstrual depression (see p53), although the evidence for this is inconclusive. St John's Wort and hypericum are herbal extracts that have often been used to treat depression. The most convincing evidence was for St John's Wort. However, when rigorous studies were conducted, the evidence did not support its effectiveness. The problems with natural substances are that they do not receive the same scientific scrutiny as conventional medicines; side-effects are not as well known or documented; and because dosages are not established scientifically, there is the risk of adverse effects from taking too much.

How can exercise treat depression?

Intense physical exercise very often gives people an enhanced sense of well-being. Going for a 5-mile run, for example, can make you feel better for the rest of the day. Whether you run or work out in the gym, the important factor seems to be the intensity of the exercise. Studies suggest that intense exercise causes the body to release chemicals, such as endorphins, that make you feel better.

What happens if I can't do intense exercise?

This is a very common problem – most people struggle to do intense exercise on a regular basis. And those who can, may lose the ability as they get older or sustain an injury. Some people in this position might feel stuck, as they have never previously sought conventional medical help for depression; however many people, who previously relied on exercise, make the transition to conventional medical help by necessity.

Why do I lose interest in exercise when I'm depressed?

This is one of the main problems with depression: it lessens the will to seek help. Disinterest and lack of energy are strong forces that can prevent you from pursuing the things that will help you – especially if those things require effort.

Do doctors recommend diet and exercise in the treatment of depression?

Some do and some don't. If you ask your doctor, he or she will give you an opinion about your specific case. Some doctors don't recommend diet and exercise because they have found that most people don't get any benefit. This may be because people often do not stick to a diet or exercise regime long enough for them to work in depression – doctors don't like to recommend treatments that tend to fail.

Relaxation

Q Does deep relaxation help depression?

Deep relaxation can help to relieve the anxiety that often accompanies depression. It can also help stress-related somatic problems, such as headaches and backaches. Relieving anxiety can take the edge off depression and make life more comfortable.

Q How can I learn to relax?

Relaxation CDs are available in many bookstores or online. There is also a simple relaxation exercise you can try shown on p127. Relaxation exercises require practice for them to work, but people who become good at them can often achieve deep relaxation quickly and discreetly, even in the presence of others. Some people choose to listen to relaxation CDs near bedtime, especially if they have difficulty sleeping. Other ways in which people relax include massage, meditation, and yoga.

Q What is biofeedback and how can it help?

Biofeedback is a mind-body therapy that can teach you how to relax. It involves monitoring aspects of your physical state such as your heart rate, blood pressure, skin temperature, and muscle tension. This information is fed back to you by a device so that you can monitor when you are becoming more relaxed (indicated by a drop in heart rate, blood pressure, and muscle tension). As you become more aware of your internal physical state, you learn to control it consciously, so that with practice you can relax at will. Biofeedback can be useful if you are not aware of the bodily sensations of relaxation, such as warmth and heaviness.

DEEP RELAXATION

There are various techniques for relaxing your body, but these 10 steps have worked for many people. Practise the exercise for between 30–60 minutes every day or just 3 times a week. Once you master the technique, you can use it in almost any situation.

① Find a place where you will not be disturbed or distracted, especially by sudden sounds.

② Get into a comfortable position. While you are learning the technique, a sitting position is preferable to lying, as it is less likely that you will fall asleep.

③ Close your eyes. Focus on your internal state. Ignore any distractions.

④ Take some deep breaths.

⑤ Focus on your lower legs. Try to feel a sense of warmth in them. Let your legs relax. Feel their heaviness. Achieving this warm, heavy, relaxed feeling can take a few minutes at first.

⑥ Feel a sense of warmth and heaviness in your thighs.

⑦ Feel a sense of warmth and heaviness in your pelvis, abdomen, back, and chest.

⑧ Feel a sense of warmth and heaviness in your hands, forearms, arms, and shoulders.

⑨ Feel a sense of warmth and heaviness in your neck, face, and scalp.

⑩ Between practice sessions, try to relax your body – or a part of your body – in various situations. Try to use deep relaxation in everyday life. Practise it when you are falling asleep or waiting for the bus, for example.

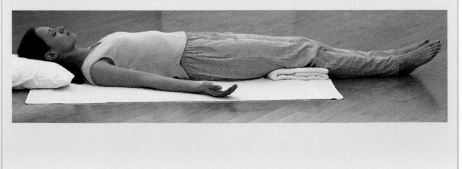

Psychological help

Together with antidepressant
medication, psychological help
in the form of psychotherapy is a
mainstay of treatment for depression.
You may receive psychotherapy
from a psychiatrist, psychologist,
psychotherapist, or counsellor.
Different types of psychotherapy use
different therapeutic techniques. A
commonly used type of psychotherapy
in the treatment of depression is
cognitive-behavioural therapy.

Seeking psychological help

Q How can I decide between different kinds of professional help for my depression?

You are faced with a very common problem. Factors to include in your decision are the kinds of professionals in your area, their cost – if any – and, most essential, your particular needs. Your best approach might be talking to friends who have had therapy, and, most importantly, to your doctor, who has the greatest experience of putting patients in touch with people who can help. Your doctor also tends to know the widest range of professionals in your area.

Q What is the difference between a psychiatrist and a psychologist?

The simple answer is that a psychiatrist is a medical doctor who specializes in mental healthcare. This means that he or she can prescribe medication as well as practise psychotherapy. A psychologist has studied psychology and is trained to practise psychotherapy, but he or she cannot prescribe medication. In my opinion, the differences are much greater, as medical doctors have had exposure to a wide variety of medical conditions and have the experience of making decisions affecting life and death. Other practitioners are likely to have their own opinions as to what the critical differences are.

Q What is psychotherapy?

Psychotherapy – or simply "therapy" – is an umbrella term for the different types of talking therapy that exist to treat psychological problems. The 2 main types of psychotherapy include the psychodynamic approach (see pp140–141) and cognitive-behavioural therapy (see pp136–139).

Q Aren't people who get professional help crazy?

Not at all. Some might be psychotic, to a greater or lesser degree, but the vast majority of people who use professional psychological help are far from crazy. People might sometimes say of someone, "he needs professional help" or "he's crazy", to be disparaging in a joking way, but the reality is that people at all levels of society seek professional help at various times in their lives. This help may be sought from lawyers, accountants, politicians, and doctors; it may equally well include psychiatrists, psychologists, or psychotherapists.

Q Is there still a stigma attached to seeking therapy?

Seeking help for psychological problems is not stigmatized in the way that it once was. The stigma tends to remain only in some cultures and subcultures. However, even if there is such a stigma, why let it stop you from getting the help you think you need? No one is entirely immune from stress-related or biological conditions that can impact upon the mind.

Q Can I take an antidepressant if I am in therapy?

You certainly can. When I first prescribed antidepressant medications to my depressed patients in therapy, I was as surprised with the fast progress they made as they were. Their rapid progress was attributable to the combination of treatments. Therapy alongside medication enables people to feel better, to understand themselves and their vulnerabilities, and to think about how to avoid psychological trouble in the future. Even when it is impossible to prevent psychological trauma – as in, say, the death of a loved one – people can at least take steps to minimize the effects of that trauma.

How psychotherapy works

Q My friend says psychotherapy is just like brainwashing. Is this true?

Your friend couldn't be further from the truth. Brainwashing is a slang term for influencing someone to think and do what the other person wants. Psychotherapy helps people remove impediments to thinking and doing what *they* want. This involves a trusting relationship between patient and therapist. It is only as this develops that patients really open up and reveal their innermost thoughts and feelings so that the therapist can help them work on these impediments.

Q How does psychotherapy work?

Different forms of psychotherapy work in different ways. However, they have certain things in common. They help the person to define and work toward goals, and to identify any impediments in reaching those goals. If irritability with your partner is a major factor in your depression, a psychotherapist will work with you to overcome this. Depending on the training and background of the therapist, you might be taught to practice relaxation techniques when you start to feel irritable; you might be encouraged to explore why your feelings of irritability arise in the first place; or you might be asked to examine ways in which you can improve interpersonal skills between you and your partner.

Q Is psychotherapy always carried out on a one-to-one basis?

Psychotherapy is often carried out on a one-to-one basis, but, depending on the nature of the problem, families and couples can also have psychotherapy. Sometimes psychotherapy takes place in a group, where all the members of the group share a similar problem.

Q I'm not very good at talking to people. Is there any point in going for psychotherapy?

This is a common reservation that people have about going for psychotherapy – many people struggle to express themselves, especially about personal problems. However, psychotherapy doesn't depend on you being articulate, good with words, or a skilled communicator. A psychotherapist is trained to be supportive and understanding, and to help you describe and understand your thoughts and feelings.

Q Can psychotherapy help me grieve?

It can help you deal with the emotions usually found in the grief response, especially those you might be having problems with. For example, if you talk to a friend about your loss and become emotional as a result, your friend may guide you away from the subject in an attempt to make you feel better – after all, why allow you to feel bad? A psychotherapist, on the other hand, knows that you must feel bad temporarily in order to feel better later.

Q Why do I have to feel bad in order to feel better?

If you have lost a loved one, you need to express your feelings about this, however painful it may be. A psychotherapist, rather than shying away from displays of emotion, will let you express them. If you stop, he or she might ask more about the loved one in order to keep you on the subject. When psychotherapy is effective in this manner, you will let all your emotions out, be they of sadness, anger, fear, guilt, or anything else. After you have expressed these emotions, they will no longer be stuck inside you and they will no longer impede your natural reaction to your loss. Once hidden blocks to this process are uncovered and dissolved, the undone emotional work can proceed, often quickly.

Myth "Psychotherapy makes you dependent. It's better to solve problems on your own"

Truth There is a healthy level of dependency that everyone must become comfortable with. If not, our success would be very limited. In our everyday lives we depend on people like lawyers, accountants, doctors, bankers, and shopkeepers. The important thing is to strike a balance between dependence and independence. One of the tasks in psychotherapy is to achieve a good balance between the two, depending on whatever situation arises. We function better if we are able to make healthy and appropriate shifts between these two poles.

Q I suffer from anxiety as well as depression. Can psychotherapy help me overcome this?

A psychotherapist can help you identify the thoughts that trigger your anxiety and encourage you to examine those thoughts. For example, are they accurate and rational? Would different thoughts help you to cope better and feel less anxious? Alternatively, you might be encouraged to understand the background to your anxiety by exploring its origins. You may also be taught practical techniques to alleviate anxiety; these might include deep breathing, muscle relaxation, or visualization.

Q My friend had psychotherapy once a week, but my therapist does it only once a month. Why the difference?

The frequency of therapy sessions partly depends on whether you are receiving treatment from the NHS or from a private therapist. Private therapy sessions may take place between 1 and 3 times a week. If you are referred for therapy under the NHS, sessions are likely to be once a week or once a month. It is advisable to ask a potential private therapist how often he or she would expect to see you, before you actually embark on therapy.

Q Does the frequency of sessions also vary according to the type of therapy?

Yes. Some types of therapy are more intensive than others. For example, if you are having psychodynamic psychotherapy, you may see your therapist up to 3 times a week, but if you are having cognitive-behavioural therapy, sessions may be held just once a week.

Q How long will I have to go for psychotherapy?

This depends partly on who is funding the psychotherapy, the nature of your problem, and what you hope to achieve. It also depends on the type of psychotherapy you are having. For example, psychodynamic psychotherapy can last for years, whereas interpersonal therapy (see p142) is generally short-term, for example, only about 16 sessions long.

Cognitive-behavioural therapy (CBT)

Q What is cognitive-behavioural therapy?

It is a type of psychotherapy based on the idea that psychological problems, such as depression, are linked to a maladaptive style of thinking. The aim of cognitive behavioural therapy (CBT) is to recognize this style of thinking and change it to a more positive one.

Q Where did CBT come from?

CBT was pioneered by the American psychiatrist Aaron T. Beck in the 1960s. Beck coined the term "automatic thoughts" to describe the reflexive thoughts that can trigger specific emotional states such as despondency or anxiety. By becoming more aware of these automatic thoughts, we can question their validity.

Q How does thinking differently help?

Our thoughts have a direct impact on our feelings and behaviour. For example, if you think: "Everyone finds me ugly," it is likely to make you feel despondent and worthless. This, in turn, impacts on your behaviour – for example, you might turn down social invitations. If you think more positively, you will feel and behave better.

Q What is the difference between CBT and positive thinking?

CBT offers a rigorous method of identifying specific thoughts and the impact they have upon the way you feel and behave. You can test out alternative thoughts to see whether they provide a more valid or accurate account of situations or events. Simply trying to "think positively" doesn't have the same benefit because it doesn't offer you a tried and tested way of achieving positive thoughts.

Q **Why would I want to change the way I think about things?**

If you are depressed, you are likely to have a depressive outlook or attitude. You may feel that everything in life is hopeless and/or that there is no point in attempting anything. If you can challenge the thoughts that have led to these feelings, you may discover that there is a more helpful, balanced, and rational way of interpreting the world. Once you adopt these more helpful interpretations, you start to feel better.

Q **What does CBT involve?**

CBT is a practical therapy that focuses on current problems. It doesn't involve detailed discussions of your unconscious motivations or analysis of things that have happened in your past. Instead, it involves discussion of the way you currently think about and interpret situations and events. By asking you questions and encouraging self-observation, your therapist will help you to identify the specific thoughts that are likely to contribute to your depression. Then he or she will explore and reflect on these thoughts, and gently encourage you to re-evaluate them. This leads you away from extreme or negative thoughts to more balanced and helpful thoughts.

Q **My therapist asked me to write down everything I did over the course of a day and then rate how satisfying each thing felt. Why?**

If you believe that you don't experience any pleasure, enjoyment, or satisfaction from anything in life, it can be helpful to discover that over the course of your day, you do actually find varying degrees of satisfaction in things. Even if pleasure or satisfaction is only rare or fleeting, this can help you to revise your belief that "I never enjoy anything". Often, it is only by rigorously recording what you do that you can discover moments of satisfaction. If you rely on memory alone, you may well remember your day as being devoid of satisfaction.

Q Do you always have to do "homework" in CBT?

Homework is an important part of CBT and may enhance the benefits of this therapy. Homework may take various forms. Your therapist may ask you to keep a diary in which you log events that make you feel depressed or anxious, and to identify and write down exactly what you were thinking and feeling at the time. You may be asked to come up with alternative thoughts that make sense of things in a less negative, more helpful way. Homework may also consist of changing your behaviour in some way. For example, going out to meet a friend for dinner, if this is something you haven't done for a while.

Q It's clear to me that life is pointless if my partner leaves me. Why does my therapist challenge this?

Your therapist will want to discover why you think that your life would be pointless if your partner leaves you. For example, it might be because you think you can't cope on your own. If this is the case, your therapist is likely to explore the validity of this thought. He or she might ask you whether you have managed to be alone at previous points in your life (before you met your current partner, for example). He or she might also challenge the idea that you would definitely be alone in the future.

Q I've failed in every job I've ever had. How can CBT make me feel less depressed about this?

Your therapist may explore your beliefs about failure with you. For example, how do you know you've failed in every job? Is it possible to identify occasions on which you didn't fail at work? How do your beliefs about failure currently impact on your life and work? Are they useful to you or have they become a self-fulfilling prophesy – in that you no longer even bother to try? Recognizing and challenging thoughts that may have become reflexive over a period of many years can help you improve your self-image.

Q Can I do CBT on myself, without going to see a therapist?

You can read about CBT and try the techniques out by yourself. You can use the example given below as a template to log your thoughts and feelings and to come up with alternative thoughts. There are also computer and CD-based CBT programs. Although self-help CBT may be useful to varying degrees, a therapist can offer you direct guidance, personal support, and encouragement. He or she can help you to define goals, recognize reflexive thoughts, challenge those thoughts, suggest new ways of behaving, and set you homework that will help you reach your goals.

Q Will CBT carry on working even after I stop therapy?

It is designed to have a long-term effect on your thoughts, feelings, and behaviour. Through the discussions and exercises that you have done with your therapist, you become more aware of your own thought processes. As a result, when you have a depressive thought about something in the future, you will be more able to challenge it and come up with a helpful alternative.

EXAMPLE OF A CBT SITUATION

Activating event	You have been arguing with your partner about the future of your relationship
Negative interpretation	"My partner doesn't love me anymore"
Feeling	Lonely and helpless
Alternative interpretation	"My partner is simply as afraid of commitment as I used to be – she just needs more time"
Feeling	Involved and more trusting

Psychoanalysis

Q What is psychoanalysis?

Psychoanalysis is a technique that was pioneered by Sigmund Freud (1856–1939). Its influence still permeates much of psychotherapy, despite advances being made in the field. Freud used analogies with medicine to describe his techniques, for example: "lance the boil and the pus gets out". This refers to the painful unleashing of emotions.

Q What did Freud's psychoanalysis involve?

It was very intense. Patients had therapy for 3 or 4 days a week. They would be asked to lie down on a sofa with the therapist sitting behind them (so that the presence of the therapist would not inhibit the free expression of the patient). One of the main techniques that Freud used was free association, which involved the patient saying everything that came into his or her mind, no matter how difficult or seemingly unimportant.

Q Are Freud's techniques still used today?

Psychoanalysis has moved on greatly since Freud's time – many other key thinkers have contributed to its development. More common than psychoanalysis is psychodynamic psychotherapy – this employs psychoanalytic techniques. Some of Freud's core principles are used in psychodynamic psychotherapy. For example, the relationship between patient and therapist, and bringing repressed thoughts and feelings into conscious awareness remain important. However, Freud's perception of depression resulting from anger turned inwards is not an area of focus any more.

Q Why was the relationship between the patient and therapist important?

Freud believed that, eventually, a patient would expect a therapist to react to him or her in the same way as his or her parents (or caregivers) reacted. This idea is called transference (the patient transfers the feelings and responses of a parent onto the therapist). As a result, the patient and therapist start to re-enact the child-parent dynamics. This rekindles the patient's early ways of responding. By exploring and analysing these kinds of dynamics with a therapist, the patient comes to understand himself or herself better.

Q Why is the unconscious important in psychoanalysis?

Freud believed the primitive erotic/aggressive drives of the unconscious mind were at odds with the rules, expectations, and boundaries imposed by the society. To resolve this, people use psychological defence mechanisms such as repression, in which impulses or urges get pushed into the unconscious. A side effect of this could be anxiety or depression. Psychoanalysis aims to bring unconscious drives and motives back into consciousness. Once understood, our unconscious impediments can be disregarded.

Q How is psychodynamic psychotherapy useful for depression?

A psychodynamic psychotherapist might say that it would help you come to terms with unconscious feelings and expectations that may contribute to your depression. For example, you may have learned as a child that you would be punished for any signs of weakness or failure. As an adult, this unconsciously influences your attitude towards relationships and life in general. By exploring these issues through your relationship with a therapist, you can stop unconsciously expecting people to punish or reject you.

Other types of psychotherapy

Q I've been advised to have interpersonal therapy (IPT) for my depression. What is it?

It is a type of psychotherapy that focuses specifically on the difficulties people encounter in their personal relationships. It helps you to manage your relationships and to develop positive strategies for resolving conflict. Improving the quality of your relationships may help to lift your depression.

Q What does interpersonal therapy involve?

Interpersonal therapy is highly structured and consists of 3 phases. During the first phase, the therapist will ask you about your depression and how you are managing in your key relationships. During the second phase, the therapist will address problem areas in your relationships and suggest strategies for improving them. During the third and final phase, the emphasis is on the ending of the therapeutic relationship and the patient's reaction to this.

Q How can interpersonal therapy help my relationships?

It can help you resolve disputes in your relationships and can help during times of life when your relationships are in transition. For example, in postnatal depression IPT encourages focusing on changed relationships with spouse, in-laws, parents, and employer. It can also help you mourn after a loved one dies (with the aim of helping you to establish new relationships) and can help you improve your interpersonal skills so that you can start to build more satisfying relationships than you have done previously.

Q **What techniques will an interpersonal therapist use?**

They include supportive listening, in which the therapist listens empathically, and communication analysis, in which the therapist examines how you communicate in relationships and whether this can be improved. A therapist may also use role-playing, and encourage you to express difficult, painful, or unpleasant emotions in a safe and therapeutic environment.

Q **My therapist says that he practices person-centred therapy. What does this mean?**

Person-centred therapy is also called client-centred or Rogerian therapy. The creator of this approach, the humanistic psychologist Carl Rogers (1902–87), believed that people have a natural ability to bring about positive change in their lives. A person-centred therapist will facilitate this change by providing a positive and supportive environment in which you can talk freely.

Q **I've heard of integrative psychotherapy. What is it?**

Integrative psychotherapy (or "eclectic therapy") draws from different schools of practice. An integrative psychotherapist might use techniques from psychodynamic, cognitive-behavioural, and person-centred therapies.

Q **What does group therapy involve?**

A group of people with a common problem, such as postnatal depression, meet in the presence of one or more trained therapists. The aim is for the group to share their experiences in a supportive environment. The specific techniques used depend on the training of the therapists.

Q **How can group therapy help me?**

Group therapy can provide reassurance that there are others in a similar position to you. You can also get wide-ranging feedback from peers on issues you want to discuss, and also feel empowered by the fact that your feedback may be helping others in the group.

Finding a therapist

Q What should I look for in a therapist?

The most important issue is whether the person has experience with your particular problems and can actually help you with them. However, because depression is so common, it would be hard to find a professional psychotherapist who does *not* have experience. If you have not been referred to a therapist by a doctor, look for therapists who belong to a professional organization and check their credentials.

Q What personal qualities should I look for in a therapist?

When you meet a therapist, consider whether he or she seems understanding, will listen to you with empathy and respect, and will make you feel at ease. It is also important to feel a sense of trust – discussing personal issues can make you feel vulnerable, and you need to feel that your therapist can provide a safe and supportive environment.

Q Can I try more than one therapist and then decide?

There is no reason why you cannot do this. Although not many people do it, professionals are accepting of this when it occurs. Choosing one therapist over another is often based not just on their competence, but also on how comfortable you are with your therapist, all other things being equal.

Q Do psychotherapists have to obey a code of conduct?

Yes, he or she should obey a professional code of practice based on regulations from a body such as the British Association for Counselling and Psychotherapy (BACP). Among other things, this means acting in your best interests and respecting your confidentiality.

Can I find a good psychotherapist on the Internet?

The Internet is a huge resource pool, so you may be able to. The question is: can you find a good psychotherapist in your area? Your doctor, who knows your condition and the range of psychotherapists in your area, is generally a better source. Another potential source is friends who have had psychotherapy. However, it is important to remember that what has worked for one person may not necessarily work for you.

What happens when I think I've found a therapist?

Many therapists conduct an initial assessment session. This is a 2-way process that gives you a chance to see if you feel comfortable with the therapist, and in turn, whether he or she can work with you. During this session you can ask the therapist questions about what therapy will involve, how long it will last, and about his or her training and background. The therapist will ask you questions about your depression.

Can I go to Alcoholics Anonymous for my depression?

You can, and you should, if you have an alcohol problem. However, additional treatment beyond Alcoholics Anonymous (AA) is generally recommended, whether in the form of psychotherapy, medication, or both. AA focuses on stopping drinking – you need to do that, plus more. One difficulty you may encounter with AA is if you are taking medication for your depression. Some AA groups reject the notion of medication entirely. If your depression warrants antidepressant treatment, it is best to find an AA group that supports your use of it. Finally, you might encourage your partner to attend Al-Anon, the sister group of AA intended to provide support for close relatives of people with alcohol problems.

Medical treatment

Although psychiatry still lags behind the rest of medicine in terms of scientific diagnosis and treatment, there have been many advances in the treatment of depression. There is a range of antidepressants and anxiety-reducing medications that can help, and, in some cases, electroconvulsive therapy is a useful treatment for depression.

Taking antidepressants

Q Do I have to take an antidepressant for my depression?

Not at all. Depression almost always goes away with time. If your depression does not bother you much and does not greatly interfere with your life, there is no mandate to use medication. Even in the case of a major depressive episode, many people do not use medication of any sort.

Q How bad would my depression have to be to take antidepressants?

If your depression is not severe, it is a matter of preference. Even in a really bothersome depression, if the symptoms and signs of major depression are not met, there is no clear indication that an antidepressant would even help you. However, if you have a major depressive episode that is bothering you and interfering with your work or home life, you may want to ask your doctor for antidepressant medication. If your sleep is significantly disrupted, your doctor might offer you a sleeping pill.

Q My depression is not severe, but I'd still like to try antidepressants. Is there any problem with this?

In the past, antidepressants had many side effects, and both doctor and patient did not use them in mild and even moderate cases of depression. However, since the development of SSRIs (see pp153–159), antidepressant medication is relatively free from serious side effects. This changes the risk/benefit analysis in favour of treatment. The thinking has become: "If the treatment has a low chance of doing harm, and the benefits outweigh the risk of harm, why not get the benefits by using the antidepressant?" This shifting of risk/benefit analyses occurs in all medical conditions as new treatments become more and more mild.

Q How many times a day do I need to take my antidepressant?

This depends on the antidepressant, but most need to be taken only once a day. Once-a-day dosing is preferred because there is less chance that you will forget a dose.

Q How can I remember to take my antidepressant?

People often remind themselves to take their pill by placing the bottle on a night table or near where they wash – this way they see it at least once a day. Even so, people may still get confused about whether or not they have taken a pill. One way to solve this problem is to use a pill container with multiple small compartments that are labelled with days of the week.

Q Now that I take antidepressants, how often do I have to see my doctor?

In general, your appointments will be weekly until your depression begins to respond to the medication. Once you are stable, you will probably see your doctor once a month. If something stressful happens and you experience a setback, your appointments will increase until you are stable again. You are also likely to visit more frequently when you are coming off an antidepressant. This is to determine whether your depressive signs and symptoms are re-emerging. If they are, your doctor can catch this early, raise your dose again, and wait a few months.

Q My grandfather was depressed, but he lived before there were antidepressants. How would he have been treated?

Before first generation antidepressants were discovered in the 1950s, people were treated with psychotherapy, sedatives such as barbiturates, and electroconvulsive therapy (see pp182–183). Psychotherapy alone was not very effective; sedatives were a patchwork treatment; only ECT was a good treatment for depression. Your grandfather might have been treated with a combination of these or he may simply have recovered with time, as depression is generally an episodic condition.

How do antidepressants work?

With our increased knowledge of brain function, we have a much better idea of how some medications work, especially antidepressants. Basically, they affect the transmission of nerve signals from one nerve cell (neuron) to the next, right at the junction of the two, called the *synapse*. This understanding has opened up the possibility for even more discoveries about antidepressant medications.

HOW NERVE CELLS COMMUNICATE

The billions of densely connected neurons in the brain transmit weak electrical signals that travel from the body of one neuron, along its axon, to the body of the next. Where the axon reaches the body of the next neuron, rather than touching, they are separated by a tiny cleft, called the *synapse* or *synaptic cleft*.

The pre-synaptic membrane releases a chemical called a neurotransmitter, which is encapsulated in a vesicle. It then crosses the synaptic cleft and is deposited at the membrane of the next neuron's body (the postsynaptic membrane). As it crosses, the

neurotransmitter opens channels in the target cell to let through charged particles and cause the next nerve cell to fire (though some inhibit rather than excite neighbouring cells). Once the neurotransmitter has exerted its effect, it is brought back into the pre-synaptic cell by a process called "re-uptake" and the process begins again.

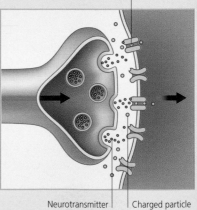

Neurotransmitters open channels in the target cell to let charged particles through

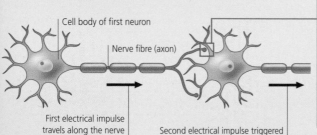

Cell body of first neuron

Nerve fibre (axon)

First electrical impulse travels along the nerve fibre to the target cell

Second electrical impulse triggered by neurotransmitter molecules

Neurotransmitter

Charged particle

NEUROTRANSMITTERS AND DEPRESSION

Certain neurotransmitters are implicated in depression, and antidepressants work by increasing the levels of these neurotransmitters. They do this by inhibiting the re-uptake process. This leaves more neurotransmitters at the postsynaptic cleft, presumably leading to more firing of the postsynaptic neuron. Neurotransmitters that have been targeted by antidepressants include serotonin, noradrenaline (also known as norepinephrine), and others. However, the problem with some types of antidepressants is that they target neurotransmitters found in parts of the brain other than the ones affected by depression. This leads to excess firing of these other neurons, which in turn leads to side effects.

Fluoxetine (Prozac) was the first antidepressant to inhibit serotonin selectively, which is why it is called a selective serotonin re-uptake inhibitor (SSRI). Because it affected only one neurotransmitter, its effects were only on those parts of the brain in which serotonin was a predominant neurotransmitter. This is why SSRIs have fewer side effects than other classes of antidepressant.

HOW SSRIs WORK

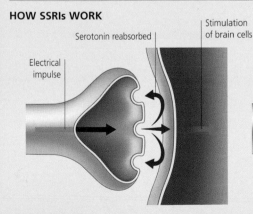

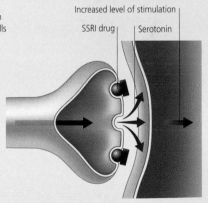

BEFORE THE DRUG *When an electrical impulse reaches the nerve ending, serotonin is released. It crosses the cleft, stimulates the next nerve cell and is then reabsorbed.*

AFTER THE DRUG *An SSRI can block the re-uptake of serotonin by occupying the exact places on the nerve ending where the molecules of serotonin would be reabsorbed.*

Myth "When you feel better, you can just stop taking an antidepressant"

Truth Unfortunately, this isn't the case. As with penicillin – which relieves a strep throat in 3 days or so, but must be taken for 10 to avoid relapse – antidepressants must be continued beyond the time you feel better. Generally, the recommended duration of treatment is 6 months, but some people will try to taper off antidepressant use in 3 months. Some doctors prefer 9 to 12 months, however, since there is a risk of relapse with shorter treatment.

Types of antidepressants

Q What are the different types of antidepressants?

The 2 main types of antidepressant are the tricyclic antidepressants (TCAs) and the selective serotonin re-uptake inhibitors (SSRIs). Fluoxetine (Prozac) is probably the most popular SSRI. There is also a third group of antidepressants (MAOIs; see p158), but they are not used often because they can have a dangerous interaction with certain types of food. There are also some miscellaneous types such as venlafaxine and duloxetine.

Q Does fluoxetine work better than the other antidepressants?

Fluoxetine revolutionized antidepressant treatment. It isn't that it works better – it just has fewer side effects. Since it does not have the same side effects as medications used by medically ill people, including the elderly, fluoxetine (as well as other SSRIs) can be used on more depressed people than other antidepressants. In fact, it is so much safer that it is used even in mild cases of depression.

Q Is it true that fluoxetine is not supposed to be used with certain medications?

Not exactly. Fluoxetine and other SSRIs block the body's clearance of some other medications, which then build up in the body until they reach toxic levels. However, as long as all your doctors know about all the medications you are taking, they can monitor and adjust the doses of these other medications accordingly. Drug-drug interactions, which is what this is called, do not prohibit use of a particular medication. As long as there is monitoring, your doctor does not have to take you off a medication that is helping you, but can just lower the dose.

Q Is fluoxetine less toxic than other antidepressants?

Fluoxetine is less toxic than the TCAs and the MAOIs. TCAs can easily cause death if patients take an overdose, but this is not the case with fluoxetine. This is why doctors are less wary of prescribing fluoxetine to depressed people who are suicidal. Another advantage of fluoxetine is that, unlike the TCAs, it does not lead to weight gain. When fluoxetine first came onto the market, there was speculation in the *Wall Street Journal* that it could be marketed as a diet pill, making it much more valuable than a mere antidepressant. Some psychiatrists joke by calling fluoxetine "vitamin P".

Q Are there any problems with fluoxetine?

Fluoxetine became so widely used that even rare problems with it were recognized. There was also some speculation that it could cause suicide. It is important to note that all antidepressant use is associated with the possibility of suicide. Suicide is considered a complication of antidepressant use in that once a depressed person's motivation and energy levels are normalized by an antidepressant, they become more able to act on the desire to commit suicide. With fluoxetine, however, it was thought that there was a risk of suicide even in people who did not fall into this pattern.

Q Should I be worried about the link between suicide and fluoxetine?

After much research, it was found that claims about a link between fluoxetine and suicide were unfounded in adults. In adolescents, however, recent information indicates that fluoxetine and the other antidepressants in the SSRI family are associated with increased suicidal thoughts and behaviour, although not with suicide itself.

Q My doctor has given me more than the recommended dose of fluoxetine. Is this okay?

Drugs are sold with recommended doses that are approved by the government. These are usually lower than the doses that doctors eventually use. This is because, to be approved, a new drug has to be safe and effective; it must work without causing many or severe side effects. For this reason, many drugs are tested at the lowest dose that works. Once the drug starts to be used, it is found that people with more challenging cases need and can tolerate higher doses. Additional studies are usually done, and the upper limit is raised. If a patient needs a higher dose and the benefits of this are not outweighed by additional side effects, a doctor will go ahead and prescribe a higher dose.

Q Are there other drugs that are similar to fluoxetine?

Yes, all the SSRIs – including fluoxetine – work in a similar manner. When fluoxetine was launched, it was such a success that other drug companies developed similar drugs that had the same action on the brain. Although these drugs are chemically different from one another, they all work on nerve receptors that respond to the neurotransmitter serotonin. They allow more serotonin to be left at the postsynaptic cell membrane by inhibiting its re-uptake by the pre-synaptic nerve cell (see pp150–151).

Q My wife's doctor said she had a chemical imbalance and gave her an SSRI to fix it. Why didn't he mention depression?

Perhaps he did not want to emphasize the overt reasons for prescribing the SSRI, so he defined your wife's depression in chemical terms. Actually, there is no evidence that depression is the result of a chemical imbalance. No one knows whether there is supposed to be more or less serotonin at the nerve cell synapse. What we do know is that medications that allow more serotonin to remain at the postsynaptic cell membrane work for depression.

Q I've been prescribed a drug called citalopram. What is it?

Citalopram (Cipramil) is an antidepressant that belongs to the SSRI class. Others in this class are sertraline (Zoloft), paroxetine (Seroxat), fluvoxamine (Faverin), and escitalopram (Cipralex), which is a purified form of citalopram. In common with the other SSRIs, citalopram may cause digestive upset, loss of appetite, and weight loss. Some people who take citalopram may experience palpitations, light-headedness on standing up, and unusual dreams. As with other SSRIs, citalopram shouldn't be stopped abruptly because symptoms such as headache, anxiety, dizziness, and sleep disturbance may result.

Q My doctor gave me trazodone to help me sleep. Isn't this an antidepressant?

Trazodone is a medication that is related to the SSRI class of antidepressants and it came onto the market as an antidepressant. Although it was effective, it never became very popular in the treatment of depression. However, because it made people sleepy, trazodone was used as a sleeping medication. Mirtazapine (Zispin), which is still used for depression, is another medication that is used to help people sleep. The same is true for doxepin, which is a TCA. It is not at all unusual for medications to start out with one use and become popular for another.

Q I have heard about an old anaesthetic medicine that reverses depression in just hours. Could this be true?

Recent studies indicate that the anaesthetic ketamine, when given intravenously, can reverse depression in as little as 2 hours. The effects of ketamine can last about a week. Ketamine would not be suitable for treating depression in its current form since it causes side effects including hallucinations and perceptual disturbances, but research may eventually lead to the development of much faster-acting antidepressants. This is under active experimentation.

DRUGS WITH MULTIPLE USES

Alert physicians, both psychiatrists and other medical specialists, are constantly finding new uses for existing drugs. Some of the following examples are established treatments, while others are still experimental.

USE OF OTHER MEDICATIONS IN TREATING DEPRESSION

USE IN DEPRESSION	MEDICATION	ORIGINAL USE
Sleep	Diphenhydramine	Antihistamine
	Trazodone	Antidepressant
	Doxepin	Antidepressant
Antidepressant	Imipramine	Tuberculosis
	Ketamine	Anaesthetic
Bipolar depression	Oxcarbazepine	Epilepsy
	Divalproex	Epilepsy
	Carbamazepine	Epilepsy
	Lamotrigine	Epilepsy
	Topiramate	Epilepsy
Anxiety	Hydroxyzine	Antihistamine
Erectile dysfunction	Sildenafil	Antihypertensive

USE OF ANTIDEPRESSANTS IN TREATING OTHER CONDITIONS

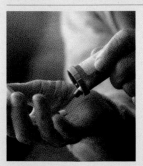

CONDITION	ANTIDEPRESSANT
Enuresis	Imipramine
Smoking	Bupropion
ADD/ADHD	Imipramine, SSRIs
Pain	Amitriptyline, SSRIs
Anxiety disorders	SSRIs, imipramine
Primary insomnia	Trazodone, doxepin

TYPES OF ANTIDEPRESSANTS

TYPE	EXAMPLES	TIMING OF DOSE
MAOI Monamine oxidase inhibitor: blocks breakdown of serotonin and noradrenergic neurotransmitters	• Phenelzine • Isocarboxazid • Tranylcypromine • Moclobemide	• Variable: can be divided in doses or taken once a day
TCA Tricyclic and tetracyclic antidepressant: blocks re-uptake of the neurotransmitters serotonin and noradrenaline	• Amitriptyline • Imipramine • Doxepin • Nortriptyline • Clomipramine	• Bedtime
SSRI Selective seroton re-uptake inhibitor: blocks re-uptake of the neurotransmitter serotonin	• Fluoxetine • Sertraline • Paroxetine • Fluvoxamine • Citalopram • Escitalopram	• Once a day: morning if energizing, bedtime if sedating
Other Blocks various neurotransmitters	• Venlafaxine • Mirtazepine • Trazodone • Duloxetine	• Varies

POSSIBLE SIDE EFFECTS	COMMENTS
• Dangerous reaction if taken with certain types of food and medicines	• Works well when panic or anxiety is present • Less popular than SSRIs due to side effects
• Sleepiness • Weight gain • Lightheadedness on rising • Blurry visions • Constipation • Difficulty urinating • Sweating • Toxic in overdose	• Few advantages over other classes of antidepressant – less popular currently due to side effects • Doxepin used as a sleep medication • Amitriptyline used for chronic pain
• Sexual dysfunction • Inhibits breakdown of various medications • Upset stomach	• Generally first choice due to minimal serious side effects • Not linked with weight gain • Less toxic in overdose • Also works for anxiety and obsessive compulsive disorder
• Variable, but not as serious as TCAs	• Second line treatment to SSRIs • Good for anxiety (venlafaxine) • Used only for sleep currently (trazodone) • Can help complaints such as stress incontinence (duloxetine)

Side effects of antidepressants

Q What does it mean when a drug is said to have side effects?

A side effect, sometimes called an adverse reaction, is a negative, unwanted effect of a treatment. All medications have side effects; they range from very benign, such as a mild upset stomach, to severe. In the worst cases, a side effect of a medication may be death.

Q My doctor finally found an antidepressant that worked for me, but it has side effects. Why aren't there medications without side effects?

Pharmaceutical companies are certainly trying to create medications that are free from side effects, using very sophisticated techniques to screen out side effects. One such technique was used with the antidepressant citalopram. Researchers were successful in purifying one of the two mirror image molecular structures in order to eliminate even mild side effects. The result was a drug called escitalopram, but, despite such purity, it still does have some mild side effects.

Q I took an antidepressant and became manic. I was later diagnosed with bipolar disorder. Was that a side effect of the drug?

This is a complication rather than a side effect. Complications tend to be occasional problems associated with a disease. For example, someone with diabetes can develop severe infection. In your case, it seems you already had bipolar disorder when you were prescribed the antidepressant, which had the effect of lifting your mood into mania. This would not be considered a side effect; it could have occurred no matter what medication was administered, and it generally derives from the disease itself rather than from the treatment.

Q How can doctors justify giving medications that can cause serious side effects?

Young doctors often have a problem with this. Then, they realize that if they don't proceed with treatment, the result may be worse. This is called a risk-benefit analysis, and it is at the heart of every treatment decision. The question is whether the benefit outweighs the risk. For example, if the chance of a serious side effect is 10 per cent, but the chance of serious deterioration or death without treatment is 20 per cent, then a doctor would make the decision to go ahead with the treatment. These are not easy decisions to make, as the probabilities are generally not so clear. Making decisions about treatment is a part of the art of medicine.

Q What side effects do antidepressants usually have?

The first generation of antidepressants, which included tricyclic antidepressants (TCAs), were associated with side effects such as blurry vision, weight gain, lightheadedness on rising, and constipation. There was no good way to work around these side effects and elderly patients, or those on medication for medical problems, could not take these antidepressants. Then came fluoxetine (Prozac), which did not have these side effects. This enabled older people and those on a variety of other medications to use it. Fluoxetine could be prescribed even in cases of mild or moderate depression – all because of its low side-effect profile.

Q Do SSRIs, such as fluoxetine, have any side effects?

The SSRIs have far fewer side effects than tricyclic antidepressants – the main side effects are sex-related (see pp163–166). Secondary side effects, such as nausea, tend to be mild or go away with continued use. Nausea can be diminished by taking the antidepressant at meal times.

Myth "Antidepressants cause addiction"

Truth While any medication, behaviour, or even food can produce a craving called psychological addiction, very few produce true physiological addiction. True addiction is characterized by tolerance (needing an increasing amount of medication to achieve the same effect), and withdrawal symptoms if the medication is stopped. This can occur with alcohol, tranquillizers, and narcotics. Antidepressants do not do this. This doesn't mean, however, that antidepressants do not have other possible side effects.

Q Are side effects ever beneficial?

Yes, they can be. For example, if your depression makes your energy levels low, then an antidepressant that can cause mild agitation might be a good choice. Similarly, antidepressants that tend to make people sleepy would be beneficial to those who have sleep problems.

Q When my friend took an antidepressant at night, it wired him up. Should he stop it?

Not necessarily. If your friend's depression makes his energy levels very low, an antidepressant that activates him can be helpful if it is taken in the morning rather than the evening.

Q Do some medications have antidepressant side effects?

Yes, they do. Interestingly, one of the first and most popular of the early antidepressants – imipramine – started life as a drug for tuberculosis. When people with chronic tuberculosis were given a trial of imipramine, many of them felt significantly better. At first, it was thought that their tuberculosis had improved. However, it turned out that those who felt better had been depressed (not uncommon for people with chronic illnesses) and imipramine had had an antidepressant side effect. This led to its use as an antidepressant, rather than an antituberculosis medicine.

Q Do antidepressants affect male sex drive?

Just as depressed people lose interest in other things, they may have little or no interest in sex. Once antidepressants begin to take effect, sexual interest usually re-emerges. However, some antidepressants, especially the SSRIs, diminish sex drive. Men tend not to complain about this if, as a result of depression, they have lost interest in sex. They may assume that the medication is yet to bring about an improvement. Men who are more likely to complain are those who haven't lost their sex drive due to depression.

Q Do antidepressants affect a man's ability to have sex?

Besides diminishing sex drive, antidepressants, such as SSRIs, can also diminish sexual function. This means that you might find it difficult to get an erection or ejaculate, although some antidepressants have been found to cause prolonged erections. People who find this most upsetting are those who have not lost their sex drive due to depression. If you are forewarned about the sex-related side effects of antidepressants, you can let your doctor know if you begin to experience them and then the problems can be worked around.

Q Why won't my teenage son take his antidepressant? He says it affects his relationships.

It is likely that the antidepressant is affecting his sexual function. This is a touchy subject, especially for young people. It is important for doctors to prepare patients for a variety of side effects – your son needed to be warned and told that the sexual problems could have been worked around. The result you describe happens all too often because of a lack of communication between a doctor and patient.

Q I'm having sexual problems, and I take a variety of medications. How do I know which, if any, is responsible?

The sexual side effects of antidepressants can impact your sex drive, your sexual performance, and your sexual satisfaction. But many other medications can also cause these side effects, so you will probably need them to be evaluated by a doctor who will sift out the effects of each. Your doctor can point to likely culprits and advise you how to stop or substitute medications for each possible culprit in turn. Once you have identified which drug is responsible, hopefully there will be a replacement that works as well as the medication causing the problem.

Q How are sexual side effects dealt with?

There are several ways to work around the sexual side effects of antidepressants. One way is to lower the dosage of the medication. If the beneficial effects remain and the side effects are resolved, then the problem is solved. Another way is to switch to an antidepressant that tends not to have sexual side effects, such as duloxetine (Cymbalta). If the new antidepressant does not work as well as the first one, then your doctor can try adding a small amount of another antidepressant. In most cases, such problems can be solved.

Q Can I skip my antidepressant on a day when I want to have sex?

Yes, this is another strategy that people use to overcome the sexual side effects of antidepressants. Alternatively, some people hold off and take their antidepressant right after they have had sex.

Q What happens when sexual side effects can't be overcome?

In cases where sexual problems cannot be resolved, the doctor and patient are left with no choice but to carry out a risk/benefit analysis. If an improvement in depression is deemed more important than normal sexual function, then the medication is continued. If not, then it is stopped. Depression can be so bad that people will tolerate sexual side effects from a medication that works well. Of course, ECT (see pp182–183) is always available as an alternative treatment, but I have not heard of its use in cases where otherwise beneficial medication caused sexual side effects. On the horizon, emerging therapies such as transcranial magnetic stimulation, intense exercise, vagal nerve stimulation, and possibly acupuncture may be viable alternatives to drug treatments.

Q **Is it okay to take medication for erection problems as well as an antidepressant?**

It is more than okay – it is often recommended in cases where men experience the sexual side effects of antidepressant use. The medications for erectile dysfunction (problems getting or keeping an erection) are relatively safe. One of the leading reasons for erectile dysfunction is that it is a side effect of a variety of medications. Unless there is a reason not to use a medication to help erectile dysfunction, a doctor would rarely hesitate to prescribe one in such situations. However, medications such as sildenafil (Viagra) are prescription only, and you should use them only if they have been prescribed to you personally by your doctor.

Q **Antidepressants have made me last longer during sex. Can I stay on them?**

A delay in the length of time it takes to ejaculate can be a side effect of some antidepressants. This can work well for some men, particularly if they previously had problems with premature ejaculation. As to whether you can stay on the medication after your depression lifts, this would best be determined by a discussion with your doctor. At present, studies do not report specific long-term side effects due to antidepressant use, so you may be able to continue.

Q **Do women get sexual side effects from antidepressants?**

They do, but they are less likely to get them than men. The sexual side effects of antidepressants in women might be diminished sex drive, altered lubrication, or difficulty achieving orgasm. As with male sexual dysfunction, it may be possible to reduce side effects by lowering the dosage or switching antidepressants. Alternatively, lubricants or increased clitoral stimulation may help couples to work around problems.

Do antidepressants work?

Q How long does it take for an antidepressant to work?

Antidepressants are about the slowest of all the drugs for psychiatric conditions and take about 2 weeks just to show signs of working. If the starting dose fails, then a higher dose is given – you must then wait another 2 weeks to see if this dose works. Given that the dosage of the most popular antidepressants can be increased three to four times before being deemed a failure, it can take a long time just to see the beginnings of a response. This can be very frustrating, as most medications work much faster.

Q Will I just wake up one morning and feel better?

That happens, but it is rare. People who have this response are usually those who describe their depression as a black cloud. Some of them will know the day it lifts. For most people, however, the improvement is so slow that it is imperceptible. They might continue to feel bad, even though various signs and symptoms, such as sleep or appetite, normalize. Generally, it is only in retrospect that you can tell when an antidepressant began to work.

Q When an antidepressant works, does that mean I'm cured?

Antidepressant treatment continues even after one begins to feel normal since its benefits consolidate with time. If you encounter a stressor – even a mild one – right after improvement, you are likely to get depressed again, often for days, making you feel as if you are back to square one. If you were suicidal earlier, you might resume thinking about or attempting suicide. If you continue treatment for another month or two, the same stressor might lead only to a day of feeling low; if you continue for another 2 or 3 months, the stressor may easily be shrugged off.

Q **My antidepressant worked really well, so why did I feel so low when my company was taken over?**

Your response is really the rule, rather than the exception. Antidepressants can't protect you against the ups and downs of life. By relieving your depressive signs and symptoms, they just bring you back to where you were before the onset of depression; you still remain vulnerable to serious stressors.

Q **How long do I have to take my antidepressant for?**

It is important not to rush things. Generally, from the time you have a good response, you should continue with your antidepressant for 6 months to a year. When your medication is slowly reduced, you should start seeing your doctor more often so that he or she can increase the dose again if your depression re-emerges. If this happens, your doctor can also tell you how much longer to wait before trying to discontinue medication again. Some people, especially as they get older, are unable to come off antidepressants without having a relapse. In such cases, the depression has gone from episodic to chronic. Some doctors now recommend that elderly patients stay on antidepressants indefinitely because any side effects are likely to be outweighed by the risk, if medication is discontinued, of further episodes of depression.

Q **I stopped my antidepressant without telling my doctor. When my depression returned, the medicine no longer worked. Why is this?**

It is not clear why this happens. I have had patients who were on a medication for years. They might have stopped it for a variety of reasons. However, when they re-started it, it just did not work. Although this type of occurrence is not common, it is one more reason why it is so important for patients to consult their doctor before making any alterations to prescribed treatments.

Q **What happens if an antidepressant doesn't work for me?**

It is not unusual for your first antidepressant to fail. This is called treatment resistant depression, which means that your depression continues despite treatment. At this point, there are various approaches, depending on your condition, side effects, and any other medical conditions you have. Generally, there is a gradual switch to another antidepressant. Sometimes the replacement antidepressant is in the same class as the first one (for example, another SSRI); at other times the replacement is from a different class. Alternatively, if the first antidepressant works partially, a second one may be added.

Q **What happens if the second antidepressant doesn't work?**

In such cases, it is important to re-assess your depression with your doctor. Sometimes, a depressive episode is diagnosed as major depressive disorder, when it is actually a part of bipolar disorder (see pp50–52). This can be difficult to determine, as you may never have had any indication that you have bipolar disorder. However, if bipolar disorder is the correct diagnosis, then a type of medication called a mood stabilizer (see p172) may help you.

Q **What if no medications work for me?**

If you have undergone treatment with different antidepressants and you took the maximum amount of medication in each case, you should discuss your options with your doctor. You may need adjunctive medication such as thyroid hormone (see p173) or an antipsychotic medication. In cases where medication does not work in depression, electroconvulsive therapy (ECT) is a viable alternative; its success rate in depressed patients is close to 90 per cent. ECT often works where medication does not.

MYTH OR **TRUTH?**

Myth "Antidepressants cure all kinds of depression"

Truth Antidepressants can cure major depressive episodes, but they do not always work. In addition, antidepressants do not cure reactive depressions most of the time. Other treatments, such as psychotherapy, are better for reactive depressions; that is, depression caused by the reaction to a stressful event, as opposed to depression that is more biological in origin.

Q I felt better after 4 weeks of antidepressant treatment – then I crashed. What could have happened?

You have had a relapse. When a depression lifts, the benefits of antidepressants have not yet had a chance to consolidate. If stress occurs – especially one similar to the one that triggered your depression – you will feel quite depressed again. Your doctor should prepare you for a relapse when you begin to take antidepressants. As time passes in antidepressant treatment, your gains will become more solid. As is the case with a newly healed fracture, time makes the healing stronger.

Q My doctor said my antidepressant was successful, but why do I still have trouble sleeping?

If many of your depressive symptoms have lifted, your treatment can be said to be successful. However, some symptoms can take longer to go away than others (some take weeks while others take months). Technically, during this time, you are in partial or substantial remission, but not full remission. Disordered sleep is a very useful indicator for depression. Because it occurs during the night, when many other extraneous factors are not present, it can persist even when other symptoms appear to have resolved. If sleep problems remain, one should probably not stop antidepressants.

Q Is it possible that I may need to stay on antidepressants permanently?

Yes it is. Some people become chronically depressed after several episodes of major depression. In such cases, they need to take antidepressants indefinitely to control their depression. The only way to tell if your condition is chronic is to taper your antidepressant use (with your doctor's help) and see if you stay free of depression. If not, you would need to go back on medication for another few months and try to come off it later. After a few attempts, it might become clear that your depression has become chronic and will last the rest of your life without treatment.

Other tablets for depression

Q How can sleeping pills help me with my depression?

Sleeping pills help to relieve middle and terminal insomnia (see pp85–87), the main types of insomnia that are characteristic of depression.

Q I took a sleeping pill for my depression, but I still woke up in the middle of the night. What can I do?

Sleeping pills will get you to sleep, but they won't keep you asleep. Waking up in the middle of the night (middle awakening) is a sign of depression, and ultimately, it will not resolve until your depression lifts. People who need immediate relief sometimes take another sleeping pill when they wake up in the night. However, if there are less than 4 hours left before your morning wake-up time, taking a sleeping pill can give you a hangover.

Q My doctor has given me medication to help me with my anxiety as well as an antidepressant. Why both?

If anxiety is a significant part of your depression, it can be beneficial to treat it directly instead of waiting for the antidepressant to relieve both anxiety and depression. Unlike antidepressants, some medications for anxiety can be addictive. However, they work quickly and offer considerable relief; a short course in patients not at risk for addiction has become part of everyday medical practice.

Q What is a mood stabilizer?

In mania or hypomania (a milder form), there are frequent mood swings, for example, from elation to depression, within seconds. Therefore, stabilizing mood becomes important – medications that do so are called mood stabilizers. Mood stabilizers reverse all manic symptoms and signs. They also prevent a switch from depression to mania when antidepressants are used on bipolar depressed people.

Q I have bipolar disorder. Why did my doctor give me a mood stabilizer when I was depressed?

Sometimes, even in a depressive swing, mood stabilizers work very well. This appears to be the case more in certain types of bipolar disorder, although not all. In any case, if your depression is mild, it might be useful to try this. After all, mood stabilizers, when they work, are much quicker than antidepressants. The first mood stabilizer was lithium. Newer medications are now available, which are easier to take and have fewer side effects than lithium.

Q My doctor has given me a drug called lamotrigine. What is it?

Lamotrigine is a mood stabilizer that has become popular in recent years and works well for bipolar depression. Like other mood stabilizers that came after lithium, lamotrigine came to the market as an anti-seizure medication. However, after further studies, these drugs were used extensively for bipolar disorder. This is an example of a so-called "off label" use of a medication; a process that is supported by regulatory agencies when unexpected uses of medications are discovered. However, a side effect of lamotrigine is a potentially serious rash.

Q Why has my doctor given me thyroid hormone when I don't have a thyroid condition?

Even if you do not have a thyroid condition, thyroid hormone can be helpful in depression. It is given as an "add-on" or adjunctive medication to your antidepressant. However, it generally takes a few weeks to determine if the hormone will work.

Q Are there any other "add-on" medications to antidepressants?

Other adjunctive medications are lithium and atypical antipsychotics, such as risperidone. It is not known why taking these medications together with an antidepressant sometimes works, but it does.

OTHER MEDICATIONS FOR DEPRESSION

TYPE	EXAMPLES	TIMING OF DOSE
Adjunctive Used to assist antidepressants	• Lithium • Thyroid hormone • Atypical antipsychotics	• Variable
Mood stabilizers Used to stabilize mood in bipolar disorder	• Lithium • Lamotrigine • Sodium valproate • Carbamazepine	• Taken once or twice a day
Benzodiazepines (anxiolytics) Anti-anxiety medication, used to enhance GABA, an inhibitory neurotransmitter	• Diazepam • Alprazolam • Lorazepam • Clonazepam • Oxazepam	• Multiple doses throughout the day
Other anxiolytics Other types of anti-anxiety medications	• Clonidine • Hydroxyzine	• Multiple doses throughout the day
Antidepressant soporifics Used to aid sleep	• Trazadone • Doxepin • Mirtazapine	• Bedtime
Other soporifics Other types of sleep medication	• Diphenhydramine • Quetiapine • Zolpidem • Temazepam	• Bedtime
Activators Activates depressed people with severe loss of energy (anergia and lethargy) or daytime sleepiness	• Modafinil • Methylphenidate	• Not near bedtime

POSSIBLE SIDE EFFECTS	COMMENTS
• Variable	• Added when antidepressants work only partially • Used only after thorough trial of antidepressant
• Variable – most require blood tests to monitor for side effects	• Works much faster than antidepressants • All but lithium originally used for epilepsy
• Addictive in some people • Sleepiness – can be used for sleep	• Reliable anti-anxiety effect • Generally, used until antidepressants start to work
• Lowers blood pressure (clonidine) • Sleepiness (hydroxyzine)	• Non-addictive • Originated in other fields: clonidine (blood pressure) hydroxyzine (antihistamine)
• Hangover in the morning if dose is too high	• Low side effect profile • Generally not considered to add to antidepressant effect
• Hangover in the morning if dose is too high	• Possible addictive potential (zolpidem, temazepam) • Some originated in other fields: quetiapine (antipsychotic), diphenhydramine (antihistamine)
• Addictive potential (methylphenidate) • Headache, nausea, nervousness (modafinil)	• Originated in other fields: modafinil (narcolepsy) methylphenidate (ADHD)

Going into hospital

Q Should some cases of depression be treated in hospital?

When depression becomes very severe, it may be advisable to treat it in hospital. Sometimes, a person who is dangerous or terribly disrupted has to be hospitalized. Dangerousness is defined in different ways in different places, but the 3 categories of dangerousness usually involved are: dangerousness to oneself via suicide or self-destructive behaviour; dangerousness to others by hurting or killing them; and dangerousness caused by an inability to care for oneself safely in the community.

Q My neighbour was so depressed that she was walking in traffic, yet she refused to be hospitalized. Can she be forced?

Using a section of the Mental Health Act (1983), psychiatrists have the authority to force hospitalization on someone who is dangerous. This is sometimes called "sectioning" someone. There are many restrictions on this, but it is considered a valid way of dealing with people who are so depressed, for example, that they are on the verge of killing themselves. Forced hospitalization can be a difficult step for a doctor to take, but it gets easier after recognizing that some suicide cases are prevented when this is done. Many patients will later thank a psychiatrist for doing so; nevertheless their trust has been broken and they tend not to return to that psychiatrist for treatment.

Q Why are some psychiatric units locked?

The reason for this is to prevent someone who is dangerous from walking out and committing suicide or killing someone else. A locked unit provides a safe place for dangerous patients who are in crisis. Escapes do occur but they are not common (psychiatric units are not prisons and its personnel are clinicians, not police).

Q How many psychiatric units are locked?

Currently, in the UK, most psychiatric units are open, but there are locked wards for difficult and disturbed patients. If you discover the doors on your ward are locked, this doesn't necessarily mean that you can't go out. But you will need to request permission and ask a nurse to unlock the door for you.

Q I was hospitalized after antidepressants failed to work. Then my depression lifted in days. Why?

This is quite common and there are various explanations as to why this happens. One is that being in hospital takes you away from your stressors. Another is that the hospital environment is very supportive and uncritical. Yet another explanation is that your type of depression is not responsive to antidepressants, but can be helped by social and environmental change. In any given case, it can be hard to determine which factor played a role.

Q What are the advantages of hospitalization?

One advantage of hospitalization is that nurses are present all the time, so a patient's condition can be monitored round-the-clock. His or her responses to medication and other treatments can be observed and changes can be made accordingly. If a patient has a pre-existing medical condition, consultants from a variety of specialist medical backgrounds are usually available. Patients also benefit from being in the therapeutic milieu of a hospital and from taking part in group work. Ancillary treatments, such as for alcohol or substance abuse, can be worked into a patient's programme. Social workers can work with a patient's family. Finally, hospitalization enables aftercare to be designed according to the particular circumstances of a patient.

Q Will my confidentiality be protected in a hospital?

Confidentiality is and always has been given a high priority in psychiatry. All personnel are trained in policies and procedures of confidentiality. For example, you will be asked to sign a "release of information" form when you enter a psychiatric unit – this controls who is allowed to receive information about you. If an "unapproved" person calls you at the hospital, the receptionist will say something like, "I cannot confirm or deny that a person by that name is here. I will be glad to check to see if there is someone here by that name and that person has allowed us to speak to you. If so, someone will call you back." Note that the patient's presence at the hospital has not been revealed, as this could be compromising.

Q My sister needed peace and quiet, so why is she constantly involved with other patients?

Since the 1950s, the system of psychiatric care in hospitals has changed. Prior to this, peace and quiet was the norm. Patients did not interact with one another, and staying alone in a room was common. However, it became clear over time that interaction between patients had both a diagnostic and a therapeutic purpose. For example, when given a chance to interact, a person who opts for social isolation will demonstrate this by avoiding others. An overly helpful patient will demonstrate this aspect of himself or herself, as will a demanding person. These characteristics of an individual's personality are important for doctors to consider in the treatment of depression. Also, being treated in the so-called "therapeutic milieu" encourages patients to form supportive relationships and helps them retain the skills required for social interaction and communication.

Q How can interaction between patients be therapeutic?

When patients interact, they find out that they are not alone, that there is hope, and that their conditions are not the worst in the world. Group therapy offers direct feedback in lay language from other patients – this can be the best way for a person to accept feedback. Patients, who start out by spending most of the day in their rooms desiring isolation, may begin to interact socially. The therapeutic milieu of a hospital is so supportive that it is not unusual for a patient to feel better just by being there. This can make aftercare much more easy, since the doctor gets to know that antidepressants are not necessary.

Q When I visited my son in hospital, I couldn't tell the patients from the nurses. Why don't they wear uniforms?

They may in some places. In the UK, the trend has been to lower the barrier between patient and staff. The idea is that "people are just people" and they should communicate with each other as such. Doctors and nurses are present to help, rather than to exert dominance over patients. Of course, the same holds true for medical or surgical departments, where nurses do wear uniforms, but there, the patients do not have mental health issues.

Q How does a doctor decide when to discharge a patient?

The decision to discharge a patient is one of the most difficult decisions a doctor must make. Depressed patients may claim to feel better simply to get out and attempt suicide. Basically, a doctor wants to see a reversal of what brought the person into the hospital. For example, if a patient had not received treatment, have antidepressants now started to work and is there good aftercare? Often, a doctor needs to check with people who know the patient well, such as a family member. If the patient appears to be safe, and the family member thinks he or she has recovered, then the doctor discharges the patient.

Q My father is 80 and has medical problems because of which he is depressed. Can I get him into a place that can treat both?

There are psychogeriatric units in most NHS trusts. These units serve the elderly, as they have multiple medical problems. In such settings, there are doctors and nurses trained in both fields. In a psychogeriatric unit, patients need care for both their physical and psychiatric conditions.

Q Apart from hospitals, are there other types of residential care for depressed people?

There are many private residential homes for patients with long-term psychological problems. These facilities are generally not locked, nor are they as well-staffed as psychiatric units in hospitals. Sometimes it becomes clear that a person is seriously suicidal and needs hospitalization.

Q Why was I sent to my room when I was in hospital?

The appropriate reason for sending you to your room is to de-stimulate you, so you won't get upset and act inappropriately. It should never happen because a staff member doesn't like you. People with depression sometimes get so agitated or panicky with other people around, that a chance to calm down can really help them. In some cases, a patient is asked to stay in what is called a quiet room. This provides even more opportunity for de-stimulation.

Q How is my progress assessed when I am in hospital?

There is a weekly ward round in which you meet the team looking after you. This meeting is usually led by your consultant who will ask questions about how you are feeling (this may be the only occasion during the week when you see your consultant). Decisions about your progress and future care will be made on the basis of this meeting. If there are issues you would like to raise, its a good idea to make a note of them in advance.

Q **Is it true that once you're admitted to a hospital with depression it's difficult to get out?**

This is no longer the case. In the past, inpatient care continued for a very long time. In the UK, individual counties had large hospitals where they kept people who could not or would not function in the community. However, with the advent of effective treatments, the majority of these patients improved to the point where they could be discharged. Some recovered entirely, while others still needed treatment. Most county hospitals have been closed, as they are no longer needed.

Q **Why won't they let my daughter out of the hospital?**

If a doctor feels a person is still dangerous, he or she will not discharge that person. However, there are legal limits on keeping a person against his or her will. For this reason, to keep someone in hospital, a section of the Mental Health Act (1983) is used. If the section is approved, it can run for months. In most cases, the person improves long before the section ends.

PSYCHIATRIC HOSPITALIZATION

ADVANTAGES	DISADVANTAGES
Enables observation and protection from suicidal or homicidal impulses.	The costs may be prohibitive if the home is privately run.
Provides access to care for patients unable to look after themselves.	There remains a stigma to having been hospitalized psychiatrically.
Often provides opportunities for classes, recreational activities, and occupational therapy.	Can encourage patients to abdicate responsibility for treating or attempting to overcome the condition.
Allows intense evaluation of the patient's condition.	May be located some distance from the patient's family and community.

Electroconvulsive therapy

Q What is electroconvulsive therapy?

Electroconvulsive therapy (ECT) involves sending an electric current through the brain to trigger a seizure or fit. The treatment is administered in 5 to 10 seconds. To avoid side effects, the patient is given strong muscle relaxants and briefly anaesthetized during the treatment.

Q How does ECT help in depression?

The answer to this is not known. What is known is that people often have an enhanced sense of well-being after a seizure. There are anecdotes of depressed patients with epilepsy deliberately stopping their anti-seizure medication in order to trigger a seizure to feel better – for a while. This led to the development of several methods to trigger a seizure in people with depression. Electric shock was the first technique; insulin shock followed later.

Q Isn't ECT a desperation treatment?

Unfortunately, ECT has been stigmatized. It was developed before antidepressants and other medications were available. As a result, it was used for conditions that did not respond to it. Now, by selecting patients (depressives and others) who are likely to respond to it, the success rate of ECT is very high – approaching 90 per cent.

Q Is ECT dangerous?

A major reason for ECT's unpopularity is its side effects. Because seizures involve muscle contractions, there was a risk of spinal fracture in elderly patients. This risk has been almost entirely eliminated by giving a very short-acting paralytic agent during the treatment. An anaesthesiologist briefly anaesthetizes and gives the paralytic agent, and uses a bag or device to help the patient breathe.

Q My father lost his memory from ECT, so aren't there still problems with it?

Yes, there are. Short-term memory can be affected, generally for a few weeks if there are several ECT treatments in quick succession. Patients tend to lose the ability to remember new things, such as what they had for breakfast. After a few weeks, this ability returns to normal. In rare cases, it may take longer.

Q My mother had a great response to ECT, but it didn't last. Are there limits to how much ECT she can have?

The usual number of ECT treatments is between 6 to 8. Many people, however, have "maintenance ECT". This means that after their initial series of treatments, only one treatment might be given every 4 or 6 weeks. This minimizes the chance of a recurrence for someone whose depression is unresponsive to antidepressants.

Q Is ECT given only to depressed patients who are hospitalized?

While most people get their initial series of treatments during a hospital stay, subsequent treatments can be given to outpatients. The person does not eat the night before, as with other procedures requiring anaesthesia. He or she comes into the treatment room in the morning, goes through the brief anaesthesia during which the ECT treatment is given, and then leaves after the anaesthesia medications wear off, often in an hour or two.

Q If ECT is successful, can I stop taking my antidepressant?

Sometimes you can, and sometimes you cannot. During the morning of the treatment, most other medications are not taken. However, after the entire series of treatment is complete, people often need to re-start their antidepressant and other medications for depression in order to maintain the improvement from ECT.

Useful addresses

MIND (National Association for Mental Health)
PO Box 277, Manchester, M60 3XN
Info line: 0845 7660163
Website: www.mind.org.uk

Depression Alliance
212 Spitfire Studios,
63–71 Collier Street, London N1 9BE
Tel: 0845 1232320
Website: www.depressionalliance.org

Mental Health Foundation
9th Floor, Sea Containers House,
20 Upper Ground,
London, SE1 9QB
Tel: 020 7803 1101
Website: www.mentalhealth.org.uk

Relate
Herbert Gray College,
Little Church Street
Rugby, Warwickshire, CV21 3AP
Tel: 0845 456 1310
Website: www.relate.org.uk

Alcoholics Anonymous UK
PO Box 1, Stonebow House,
Stonebow, York YO1 7NJ
Tel: 01904 644026
www.alcoholics-anonymous.org.uk

MDF The Bipolar Organisation
Castle Works, 21 St George's Road
London, SE1 6ES
Tel: 08456 340 540
Website: www.mdf.org.uk

The Association for Post Natal Illness
145 Dawes Road, Fulham,
London, SW6 7EB
Tel: 020 7386 0868
Website: www.apni.org

YoungMinds
48-50 St John Street,
London EC1M 4DG
Tel: 020 7336 8445
Website: www.youngminds.org.uk

SAD Association
PO Box 989, Steyning, BN44 3HG
Website: www.sada.org.uk

Samaritans
Helpline: 08457 90 90 90
Website: www.samaritans.org

Royal College of Psychiatrists
17 Belgrave Square,
London, SW1X 8PG
Tel: 020 7235 2351
Website: www.rcpsych.ac.uk

Index

A

B

About the Author
Melvyn Lurie is an honours graduate of Harvard Medical School, where he won the Reznick Prize for excellence in research for his fellowship work at the Pasteur Institute in Paris. After completing his residency training in psychiatry at McLean Hospital, Dr Lurie remained on the Harvard Medical Faculty for over 20 years. He is the founder and former editor/publisher of *Medical & Health News* and continues writing and teaching medical students and laymen, in addition to seeing patients in the Boston, Massachusetts area. In the course of his career, Dr Lurie has treated a wide range of psychiatric conditions, performed various types of psychotherapy, and used psychopharmacology extensively. He has also acted as expert consultant on these subjects to business, government, and the legal profession.

Authors' acknowledgments
My name might be on the cover of this book, but, like most projects, it is the result of a team effort. First, I would like to thank my editors at DK: Kesta, Pip, Tom, and Adèle. Next, a big thank you to the models who posed for the photos. Finally, and most of all, I would like to thank my patients and their families, who have shown me that, with their perseverance, the treatments for depression really do work.

I would like to dedicate this book to my four really cool children.

For the publishers
Dorling Kindersley would like to thank Ann Baggaley for additional editorial assistance; Isabel de Cordova and Kathryn Wilding for additional design assistance; and Jo Walton for help with picture research.

Picture credits
The publisher would like to thank the following for their kind permission to reproduce their photographs (key: a-above; b-below/bottom; c-centre; l-left; r-right; t-top):

Alamy Images: BananaStock 110; Scott Camazine 7l, 162; PHOTOTAKE Inc. 6r, 128; Purestock 56; Saareli 123r; **Corbis:** Jon Feingersh 17l; Martin Harvey 121c; Jose Luis Pelaez, Inc. 152, 157, 170; LWA-Dann Tardif 146; Roy Morsch 123l; Tim Pannell 121l; Steve Prezant 100; Norbert Schaefer 22, 40; Ariel Skelley 28; Tom Stewart 134; Allana Wesley White 7r; Larry Williams 34; A. Snyder/Photex/zefa 68; Ajax/zefa 17c; Emely/zefa 44; Mika/zefa 7c, 107; Ole Graf/zefa 78; **Getty Images:** Wendy Ashton 2; Altrendo Images 6c; Bruce Ayres 24; Clarissa Leahy/Stone 8; Donna Day 123c; David Hanover 17r; Philip Lee Harvey 38; Stuart McClymont 6l, 121r; Siri Stafford 14

All other images © Dorling Kindersley
For further information see: www.dkimages.com